Learning Bayesian Models with R

Become an expert in Bayesian machine learning
methods using R and apply them to solve real-world
Big Data problems

Dr. Hari M. Koduvely

[PACKT] open source *
PUBLISHING   community experience distilled

BIRMINGHAM - MUMBAI

Learning Bayesian Models with R

First published: October 2015

Production reference: 1231015

Published by Packt Publishing Ltd.
Livery Place
35 Livery Street
Birmingham B3 2PB, UK.

ISBN 978-1-78398-760-3

www.packtpub.com

Credits

Author
Dr. Hari M. Koduvely

Reviewers
Philip B. Graff

Nishanth Upadhyaya

Commissioning Editor
Kartikey Pandey

Acquisition Editor
Nikhil Karkal

Content Development Editor
Athira Laji

Technical Editor
Taabish Khan

Copy Editor
Trishya Hajare

Project Coordinator
Bijal Patel

Proofreader
Safis Editing

Indexer
Hemangini Bari

Graphics
Abhinash Sahu

Production Coordinator
Nitesh Thakur

Cover Work
Nitesh Thakur

About the Author

Dr. Hari M. Koduvely is an experienced data scientist working at the Samsung R&D Institute in Bangalore, India. He has a PhD in statistical physics from the Tata Institute of Fundamental Research, Mumbai, India, and post-doctoral experience from the Weizmann Institute, Israel, and Georgia Tech, USA. Prior to joining Samsung, the author has worked for Amazon and Infosys Technologies, developing machine learning-based applications for their products and platforms. He also has several publications on Bayesian inference and its applications in areas such as recommendation systems and predictive health monitoring. His current interest is in developing large-scale machine learning methods, particularly for natural language understanding.

I would like to express my gratitude to all those who have helped me throughout my career, without whom this book would not have been possible. This includes my teachers, mentors, friends, colleagues, and all the institutions in which I worked, especially my current employer, Samsung R&D Institute, Bangalore. A special mention to my spouse, Prathyusha, and son, Pranav, for their immense moral support during the writing of the book.

About the Reviewers

Philip B. Graff is a data scientist with the Johns Hopkins University Applied Physics Laboratory. He works with graph analytics for a large-scale automated pattern discovery.

Philip obtained his PhD in physics from the University of Cambridge on a Gates Cambridge Scholarship, and a BS in physics and mathematics from the University of Maryland, Baltimore County. His PhD thesis implemented Bayesian methods for gravitational wave detection and the training of neural networks for machine learning.

Philip's post-doctoral research at NASA Goddard Space Flight Center and the University of Maryland, College Park, applied Bayesian inference to the detection and measurement of gravitational waves by ground and space-based detectors, LIGO and LISA, respectively. He also implemented machine leaning methods for improved gamma-ray burst data analysis. He has published books in the fields of astrophysical data analysis and machine learning.

I would like to thank Ala for her support while I reviewed this book.

Nishanth Upadhyaya has close to 10 years of experience in the area of analytics, Monte Carlo methods, signal processing, machine learning, and building end-to-end data products. He is active on StackOverflow and GitHub. He has a couple of patents in the area of item response theory and stochastic optimization. He has also won third place in the first ever Aadhaar hackathon organized by Khosla labs.

www.PacktPub.com

Support files, eBooks, discount offers, and more

For support files and downloads related to your book, please visit
www.PacktPub.com.

Did you know that Packt offers eBook versions of every book published, with PDF
and ePub files available? You can upgrade to the eBook version at www.PacktPub.
com and as a print book customer, you are entitled to a discount on the eBook copy.
Get in touch with us at service@packtpub.com for more details.

At www.PacktPub.com, you can also read a collection of free technical articles,
sign up for a range of free newsletters and receive exclusive discounts and offers
on Packt books and eBooks.

https://www2.packtpub.com/books/subscription/packtlib

Do you need instant solutions to your IT questions? PacktLib is Packt's online digital
book library. Here, you can search, access, and read Packt's entire library of books.

Why subscribe?

- Fully searchable across every book published by Packt
- Copy and paste, print, and bookmark content
- On demand and accessible via a web browser

Free access for Packt account holders

If you have an account with Packt at www.PacktPub.com, you can use this to access
PacktLib today and view 9 entirely free books. Simply use your login credentials for
immediate access.

Table of Contents

Preface   **v**

Chapter 1: Introducing the Probability Theory   **1**

Probability distributions   **2**
Conditional probability   **6**
Bayesian theorem   **7**
Marginal distribution   **8**
Expectations and covariance   **9**
   Binomial distribution   9
   Beta distribution   10
   Gamma distribution   11
   Dirichlet distribution   12
   Wishart distribution   12
Exercises   **13**
References   **14**
Summary   **15**

Chapter 2: The R Environment   **17**

Setting up the R environment and packages   **18**
   Installing R and RStudio   18
   Your first R program   19
Managing data in R   **19**
   Data Types in R   19
   Data structures in R   20
   Importing data into R   22
   Slicing and dicing datasets   23
   Vectorized operations   24

Writing R programs   **25**
  Control structures   25
  Functions   25
  Scoping rules   26
  Loop functions   27
    lapply   28
    sapply   28
    mapply   29
    apply   29
    tapply   30
Data visualization   **30**
  High-level plotting functions   31
  Low-level plotting commands   32
  Interactive graphics functions   33
Sampling   **33**
  Random uniform sampling from an interval   34
  Sampling from normal distribution   34
Exercises   **35**
References   **35**
Summary   **36**

Chapter 3: Introducing Bayesian Inference   **37**
  Bayesian view of uncertainty   **37**
    Choosing the right prior distribution   42
     Non-informative priors   42
     Subjective priors   44
     Conjugate priors   46
     Hierarchical priors   47
    Estimation of posterior distribution   48
     Maximum a posteriori estimation   48
     Laplace approximation   49
     Monte Carlo simulations   51
     Variational approximation   57
    Prediction of future observations   59
  Exercises   **59**
  References   **60**
  Summary   **60**

Chapter 4: Machine Learning Using Bayesian Inference   **61**
  Why Bayesian inference for machine learning?   **63**
  Model overfitting and bias-variance tradeoff   **65**
  Selecting models of optimum complexity   **66**
    Subset selection   66
    Model regularization   67

Bayesian averaging	68
An overview of common machine learning tasks	70
References	72
Summary	72
Chapter 5: Bayesian Regression Models	**73**
Generalized linear regression	73
The arm package	74
The Energy efficiency dataset	74
Regression of energy efficiency with building parameters	75
Ordinary regression	77
Bayesian regression	77
Simulation of the posterior distribution	79
Exercises	81
References	81
Summary	81
Chapter 6: Bayesian Classification Models	**83**
Performance metrics for classification	84
The Naïve Bayes classifier	85
Text processing using the tm package	87
Model training and prediction	88
The Bayesian logistic regression model	91
The BayesLogit R package	93
The dataset	93
Preparation of the training and testing datasets	94
Using the Bayesian logistic model	95
Exercises	96
References	96
Summary	97
Chapter 7: Bayesian Models for Unsupervised Learning	**99**
Bayesian mixture models	100
The bgmm package for Bayesian mixture models	103
Topic modeling using Bayesian inference	105
Latent Dirichlet allocation	106
R packages for LDA	107
The topicmodels package	108
The lda package	109
Exercises	110
References	110
Summary	111

Chapter 8: Bayesian Neural Networks	**113**
Two-layer neural networks	**114**
Bayesian treatment of neural networks	**116**
The brnn R package	**118**
Deep belief networks and deep learning	**119**
Restricted Boltzmann machines	120
Deep belief networks	123
The darch R package	124
Other deep learning packages in R	126
Exercises	**127**
References	**127**
Summary	**128**
Chapter 9: Bayesian Modeling at Big Data Scale	**129**
Distributed computing using Hadoop	**130**
RHadoop for using Hadoop from R	**130**
Spark – in-memory distributed computing	**132**
SparkR	**133**
Linear regression using SparkR	**133**
Computing clusters on the cloud	**134**
Amazon Web Services	134
Creating and running computing instances on AWS	134
Installing R and RStudio	135
Running Spark on EC2	136
Microsoft Azure	137
IBM Bluemix	137
Other R packages for large scale machine learning	**137**
The parallel R package	138
The foreach R package	138
Exercises	**139**
References	**140**
Summary	**141**
Index	**143**

Preface

Bayesian inference provides a unified framework to deal with all sorts of uncertainties when learning patterns from data using machine learning models and using it for predicting future observations. However, learning and implementing Bayesian models is not easy for data science practitioners due to the level of mathematical treatment involved. Also, applying Bayesian methods to real-world problems requires high computational resources. With the recent advancements in cloud and high-performance computing and easy access to computational resources, Bayesian modeling has become more feasible to use for practical applications today. Therefore, it would be advantageous for all data scientists and data engineers to understand Bayesian methods and apply them in their projects to achieve better results.

What this book covers

This book gives comprehensive coverage of the Bayesian machine learning models and the R packages that implement them. It begins with an introduction to the fundamentals of probability theory and R programming for those who are new to the subject. Then, the book covers some of the most important machine learning methods, both supervised learning and unsupervised learning, implemented using Bayesian inference and R. Every chapter begins with a theoretical description of the method, explained in a very simple manner. Then, relevant R packages are discussed and some illustrations using datasets from the UCI machine learning repository are given. Each chapter ends with some simple exercises for you to get hands-on experience of the concepts and R packages discussed in the chapter. The state-of-the-art topics covered in the chapters are Bayesian regression using linear and generalized linear models, Bayesian classification using logistic regression, classification of text data using Naïve Bayes models, and Bayesian mixture models and topic modeling using Latent Dirichlet allocation.

The last two chapters are devoted to the latest developments in the field. One chapter discusses deep learning, which uses a class of neural network models that are currently at the frontier of artificial intelligence. The book concludes with the application of Bayesian methods on Big Data using frameworks such as Hadoop and Spark.

Chapter 1, Introducing the Probability Theory, covers the foundational concepts of probability theory, particularly those aspects required for learning Bayesian inference, which are presented to you in a simple and coherent manner.

Chapter 2, The R Environment, introduces you to the R environment. After reading through this chapter, you will learn how to import data into R, make a selection of subsets of data for its analysis, and write simple R programs using functions and control structures. Also, you will get familiar with the graphical capabilities of R and some advanced capabilities such as loop functions.

Chapter 3, Introducing Bayesian Inference, introduces you to the Bayesian statistic framework. This chapter includes a description of the Bayesian theorem, concepts such as prior and posterior probabilities, and different methods to estimate posterior distribution such as MAP estimates, Monte Carlo simulations, and variational estimates.

Chapter 4, Machine Learning Using Bayesian Inference, gives an overview of what machine learning is and what some of its high-level tasks are. This chapter also discusses the importance of Bayesian inference in machine learning, particularly in the context of how it can help to avoid important issues such as model overfit and how to select optimum models.

Chapter 5, Bayesian Regression Models, presents one of the most common supervised machine learning tasks, namely, regression modeling, in the Bayesian framework. It shows by using an example how you can get tighter confidence intervals of prediction using Bayesian regression models.

Chapter 6, Bayesian Classification Models, presents how to use the Bayesian framework for another common machine learning task, classification. The two Bayesian models of classification, Naïve Bayes and Bayesian logistic regression, are discussed along with some important metrics for evaluating the performance of classifiers.

Chapter 7, Bayesian Models for Unsupervised Learning, introduces you to the concepts behind unsupervised and semi-supervised machine learning and their Bayesian treatment. The two most important Bayesian unsupervised models, the Bayesian mixture model and LDA, are discussed.

Chapter 8, Bayesian Neural Networks, presents an important class of machine learning model, namely neural networks, and their Bayesian implementation. Neural network models are inspired by the architecture of the human brain and they continue to be an area of active research and development. The chapter also discusses deep learning, one of the latest advances in neural networks, which is used to solve many problems in computer vision and natural language processing with remarkable accuracy.

Chapter 9, Bayesian Modeling at Big Data Scale, covers various frameworks for performing large-scale Bayesian machine learning such as Hadoop, Spark, and parallelization frameworks that are native to R. The chapter also discusses how to set up instances on cloud services, such as Amazon Web Services and Microsoft Azure, and run R programs on them.

What you need for this book

To learn the examples and try the exercises presented in this book, you need to install the latest version of the R programming environment and the RStudio IDE. Apart from this, you need to install the specific R packages that are mentioned in each chapter of this book separately.

Who this book is for

This book is intended for data scientists who analyze large datasets to generate insights and for data engineers who develop platforms, solutions, or applications based on machine learning. Although many data science practitioners are quite familiar with machine learning techniques and R, they may not know about Bayesian inference and its merits. This book, therefore, would be helpful to even experienced data scientists and data engineers to learn about Bayesian methods and incorporate them in to their projects to get better results. No prior experience is required in R or probability theory to use this book.

Conventions

In this book, you will find a number of text styles that distinguish between different kinds of information. Here are some examples of these styles and an explanation of their meaning.

Code words in text, database table names, folder names, filenames, file extensions, pathnames, dummy URLs, user input, and Twitter handles are shown as follows: "The first function is `gibbs_met`."

A block of code is set as follows:

```
myMean ←function(x){
    s ←sum(x)
    l ←length(x)
    mean ←s/l
    mean
}
>x ←c(10,20,30,40,50)
>myMean(x)
[1]   30
```

Any command-line input or output is written as follows:

```
setwd("directory path")
```

New terms and **important words** are shown in bold. Words that you see on the screen, for example, in menus or dialog boxes, appear in the text like this: "You can also set this from the menu bar of RStudio by clicking on **Session | Set Working Directory**."

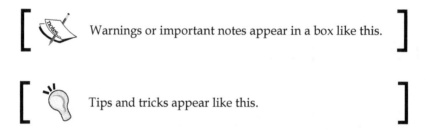

Warnings or important notes appear in a box like this.

Tips and tricks appear like this.

Reader feedback

Feedback from our readers is always welcome. Let us know what you think about this book—what you liked or disliked. Reader feedback is important for us as it helps us develop titles that you will really get the most out of.

To send us general feedback, simply e-mail feedback@packtpub.com, and mention the book's title in the subject of your message.

If there is a topic that you have expertise in and you are interested in either writing or contributing to a book, see our author guide at www.packtpub.com/authors.

Customer support

Now that you are the proud owner of a Packt book, we have a number of things to help you to get the most from your purchase.

Downloading the example code

You can download the example code files from your account at http://www. packtpub.com for all the Packt Publishing books you have purchased. If you purchased this book elsewhere, you can visit http://www.packtpub.com/support and register to have the files e-mailed directly to you.

Errata

Although we have taken every care to ensure the accuracy of our content, mistakes do happen. If you find a mistake in one of our books—maybe a mistake in the text or the code—we would be grateful if you could report this to us. By doing so, you can save other readers from frustration and help us improve subsequent versions of this book. If you find any errata, please report them by visiting http://www.packtpub. com/submit-errata, selecting your book, clicking on the **Errata Submission Form** link, and entering the details of your errata. Once your errata are verified, your submission will be accepted and the errata will be uploaded to our website or added to any list of existing errata under the Errata section of that title.

To view the previously submitted errata, go to https://www.packtpub.com/books/ content/support and enter the name of the book in the search field. The required information will appear under the **Errata** section.

Piracy

Piracy of copyrighted material on the Internet is an ongoing problem across all media. At Packt, we take the protection of our copyright and licenses very seriously. If you come across any illegal copies of our works in any form on the Internet, please provide us with the location address or website name immediately so that we can pursue a remedy.

Please contact us at copyright@packtpub.com with a link to the suspected pirated material.

We appreciate your help in protecting our authors and our ability to bring you valuable content.

Questions

If you have a problem with any aspect of this book, you can contact us at questions@packtpub.com, and we will do our best to address the problem.

Introducing the Probability Theory

Bayesian inference is a method of learning about the relationship between variables from data, in the presence of uncertainty, in real-world problems. It is one of the frameworks of probability theory. Any reader interested in Bayesian inference should have a good knowledge of probability theory to understand and use Bayesian inference. This chapter covers an overview of probability theory, which will be sufficient to understand the rest of the chapters in this book.

It was Pierre-Simon Laplace who first proposed a formal definition of probability with mathematical rigor. This definition is called the *Classical Definition* and it states the following:

> *The theory of chance consists in reducing all the events of the same kind to a certain number of cases equally possible, that is to say, to such as we may be equally undecided about in regard to their existence, and in determining the number of cases favorable to the event whose probability is sought. The ratio of this number to that of all the cases possible is the measure of this probability, which is thus simply a fraction whose numerator is the number of favorable cases and whose denominator is the number of all the cases possible.*

> *Pierre-Simon Laplace, A Philosophical Essay on Probabilities*

What this definition means is that, if a random experiment can result in N mutually exclusive and equally likely outcomes, the probability of the event A is given by:

$$P(A) = \frac{N_A}{N}$$

Here, N_A is the number of occurrences of the event A.

To illustrate this concept, let us take a simple example of a rolling dice. If the dice is a fair dice, then all the faces will have an equal chance of showing up when the dice is rolled. Then, the probability of each face showing up is $1/6$. However, when one rolls the dice 100 times, all the faces will not come in equal proportions of $1/6$ due to random fluctuations. The estimate of probability of each face is the number of times the face shows up divided by the number of rolls. As the denominator is very large, this ratio will be close to $1/6$.

In the long run, this classical definition treats the probability of an uncertain event as the relative frequency of its occurrence. This is also called a **frequentist** approach to probability. Although this approach is suitable for a large class of problems, there are cases where this type of approach cannot be used. As an example, consider the following question: *Is Pataliputra the name of an ancient city or a king?* In such cases, we have a degree of belief in various plausible answers, but it is not based on counts in the outcome of an experiment (in the Sanskrit language *Putra* means son, therefore some people may believe that Pataliputra is the name of an ancient king in India, but it is a city).

Another example is, *What is the chance of the Democratic Party winning the election in 2016 in America?* Some people may believe it is $1/2$ and some people may believe it is $2/3$. In this case, probability is defined as the **degree of belief** of a person in the outcome of an uncertain event. This is called the **subjective** definition of probability.

One of the limitations of the classical or frequentist definition of probability is that it cannot address subjective probabilities. As we will see later in this book, Bayesian inference is a natural framework for treating both frequentist and subjective interpretations of probability.

Probability distributions

In both classical and Bayesian approaches, a probability distribution function is the central quantity, which captures all of the information about the relationship between variables in the presence of uncertainty. A probability distribution assigns a probability value to each measurable subset of outcomes of a random experiment. The variable involved could be discrete or continuous, and univariate or multivariate. Although people use slightly different terminologies, the commonly used probability distributions for the different types of random variables are as follows:

- **Probability mass function (pmf)** for discrete numerical random variables
- **Categorical distribution** for categorical random variables
- **Probability density function (pdf)** for continuous random variables

One of the well-known distribution functions is the normal or Gaussian distribution, which is named after Carl Friedrich Gauss, a famous German mathematician and physicist. It is also known by the name *bell curve* because of its shape. The mathematical form of this distribution is given by:

$$N(x;\mu,\sigma) = \frac{1}{\sqrt{2\pi\sigma^2}} e^{-\frac{(x-\mu)^2}{2\sigma^2}}$$

Here, μ is the mean or location parameter and σ is the standard deviation or scale parameter (σ^2 is called variance). The following graphs show what the distribution looks like for different values of location and scale parameters:

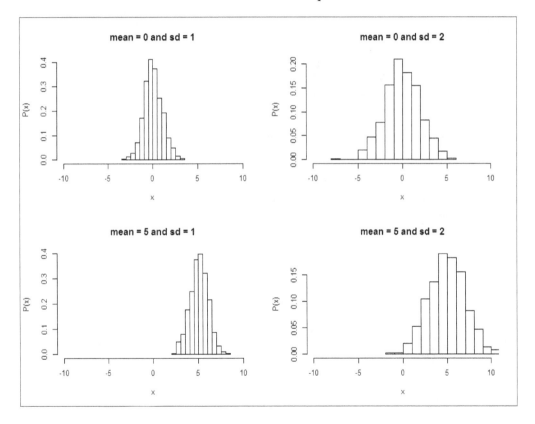

One can see that as the mean changes, the location of the peak of the distribution changes. Similarly, when the standard deviation changes, the width of the distribution also changes.

Many natural datasets follow normal distribution because, according to the **central limit theorem**, any random variable that can be composed as a mean of independent random variables will have a normal distribution. This is irrespective of the form of the distribution of this random variable, as long as they have finite mean and variance and all are drawn from the same original distribution. A normal distribution is also very popular among data scientists because in many statistical inferences, theoretical results can be derived if the underlying distribution is normal.

Now, let us look at the multidimensional version of normal distribution. If the random variable is an N-dimensional vector, x is denoted by:

$$x = [x_1, x_2, \cdots, x_N]$$

Then, the corresponding normal distribution is given by:

$$N(x \mid \mu, \Sigma) = \frac{1}{\sqrt{(2\pi)^N |\Sigma|}} exp\left(-\frac{1}{2}(x-\mu)^T \Sigma^{-1}(x-\mu)\right)$$

Here, μ corresponds to the mean (also called location) and Σ is an $N \times N$ covariance matrix (also called scale).

To get a better understanding of the multidimensional normal distribution, let us take the case of two dimensions. In this case, $x = [x_1, x_2]$ and the covariance matrix is given by:

$$\Sigma = \begin{bmatrix} \sigma_1^2 & \rho\sigma_1\sigma_2 \\ \rho\sigma_2\sigma_1 & \sigma_2^2 \end{bmatrix}$$

Here, σ_1^2 and σ_2^2 are the variances along x_1 and x_2 directions, and ρ is the correlation between x_1 and x_2. A plot of two-dimensional normal distribution for $\sigma_1^2 = 9$, $\sigma_2^2 = 4$, and $\rho = 0.8$ is shown in the following image:

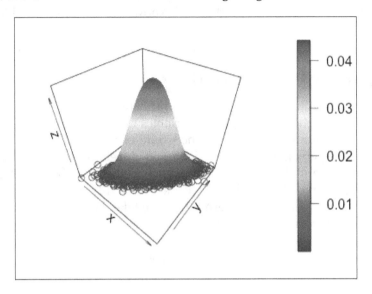

If $\rho = 0$, then the two-dimensional normal distribution will be reduced to the product of two one-dimensional normal distributions, since Σ would become diagonal in this case. The following 2D projections of normal distribution for the same values of σ_1^2 and σ_2^2 but with $\rho = 0.8$ and $\rho = 0.0$ illustrate this case:

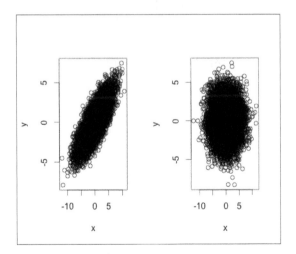

The high correlation between x and y in the first case forces most of the data points along the 45 degree line and makes the distribution more anisotropic; whereas, in the second case, when the correlation is zero, the distribution is more isotropic.

We will briefly review some of the other well-known distributions used in Bayesian inference here.

Conditional probability

Often, one would be interested in finding the probability of the occurrence of a set of random variables when other random variables in the problem are held fixed. As an example of population health study, one would be interested in finding what is the probability of a person, in the age range 40-50, developing heart disease with high blood pressure and diabetes. Questions such as these can be modeled using conditional probability, which is defined as the probability of an event, given that another event has happened. More formally, if we take the variables A and B, this definition can be rewritten as follows:

$$P(A \mid B) = \frac{P(A, B)}{P(B)}$$

Similarly:

$$P(B \mid A) = \frac{P(A, B)}{P(A)}$$

The following Venn diagram explains the concept more clearly:

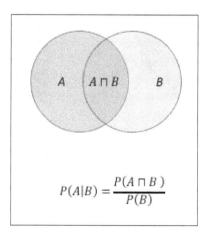

In Bayesian inference, we are interested in conditional probabilities corresponding to multivariate distributions. If $[x_1, x_2, \cdots, x_N, z_1, z_2, \cdots, z_M]$ denotes the entire random variable set, then the conditional probability of $[x_1, x_2, \cdots, x_N]$, given that $[z_1, z_2, \cdots, z_M]$ is fixed at some value, is given by the ratio of joint probability of $[x_1, x_2, \cdots, x_N, z_1, z_2, \cdots, z_M]$ and joint probability of $[z_1, z_2, \cdots, z_M]$:

$$P(x_1, x_2, \cdots, x_N \mid z_1, z_2, \cdots, z_M) = \frac{P(x_1, x_2, \cdots, x_N, z_1, z_2, \cdots, z_M)}{P(z_1, z_2, \cdots, z_M)}$$

In the case of two-dimensional normal distribution, the conditional probability of interest is as follows:

$$P(x_1 \mid x_2) = \frac{N(x_1, x_2)}{N(x_2)}$$

It can be shown that (exercise 2 in the *Exercises* section of this chapter) the RHS can be simplified, resulting in an expression for $P(x_1 \mid x_2)$ in the form of a normal distribution again with the mean $\tilde{\mu} = \mu_1 + \rho \frac{\sigma_1}{\sigma_2}(x_2 - \mu_2)$ and variance $\tilde{\sigma} = (1 - u^2)\sigma_1^2$.

Bayesian theorem

From the definition of the conditional probabilities $P(A \mid B)$ and $P(B \mid A)$, it is easy to show the following:

$$P(A \mid B) = \frac{P(B \mid A)P(A)}{P(B)}$$

Rev. Thomas Bayes (1701–1761) used this rule and formulated his famous Bayes theorem that can be interpreted if $P(A)$ represents the initial degree of belief (or prior probability) in the value of a random variable A before observing B; then, its posterior probability or degree of belief after accounted for B will get updated according to the preceding equation. So, the Bayesian inference essentially corresponds to updating beliefs about an uncertain system after having made some observations about it. In the sense, this is also how we human beings learn about the world. For example, before we visit a new city, we will have certain prior knowledge about the place after reading from books or on the Web.

However, soon after we reach the place, this belief will get updated based on our initial experience of the place. We continuously update the belief as we explore the new city more and more. We will describe Bayesian inference more in detail in *Chapter 3, Introducing Bayesian Inference.*

Marginal distribution

In many situations, we are interested only in the probability distribution of a subset of random variables. For example, in the heart disease problem mentioned in the previous section, if we want to infer the probability of people in a population having a heart disease as a function of their age only, we need to integrate out the effect of other random variables such as blood pressure and diabetes. This is called **marginalization**:

$$P(x_1, x_2, \cdots x_M) = \int P(x_1, x_2, \cdots x_M, x_{M+1}, \cdots x_N) dx_{M+1} \cdots dx_N$$

Or:

$$P(x_1, x_2, \cdots x_M) = \int P(x_1, x_2, \cdots x_M \mid x_{M+1}, \cdots x_N) P(x_{M+1}, \cdots x_N) dx_{M+1} \cdots dx_N$$

Note that marginal distribution is very different from conditional distribution. In conditional probability, we are finding the probability of a subset of random variables with values of other random variables fixed (conditioned) at a given value. In the case of marginal distribution, we are eliminating the effect of a subset of random variables by integrating them out (in the sense averaging their effect) from the joint distribution. For example, in the case of two-dimensional normal distribution, marginalization with respect to one variable will result in a one-dimensional normal distribution of the other variable, as follows:

$$N(x_1) \quad \int N(x_1 \ x_2) dx_2$$

The details of this integration is given as an exercise (exercise 3 in the *Exercises* section of this chapter).

Expectations and covariance

Having known the distribution of a set of random variables $x = \{x_1, x_2, \cdots, x_N\}$, what one would be typically interested in for real-life applications is to be able to estimate the average values of these random variables and the correlations between them. These are computed formally using the following expressions:

$$\mathbb{E}[x_i] = \int x_i \ P(x_1, x_2, \cdots, x_i, \cdots x_N) dx_1 \cdots dx_N$$

$$\sigma(x_i, x_j) = \mathbb{E}\left[(x_i - \mathbb{E}[x_i])(x_j - \mathbb{E}[x_j])\right]$$

For example, in the case of two-dimensional normal distribution, if we are interested in finding the correlation between the variables x_1 and x_2, it can be formally computed from the joint distribution using the following formula:

$$\rho = \int x_1 * x_2 N(x_1, x_2) dx_1 dx_2 - \int x_1 N(x_1) dx_1 - \int x_2 N(x_2) dx_2$$

Binomial distribution

A binomial distribution is a discrete distribution that gives the probability of heads in n independent trials where each trial has one of two possible outcomes, heads or tails, with the probability of heads being p. Each of the trials is called a Bernoulli trial. The functional form of the binomial distribution is given by:

$$P(k; n, p) = \frac{n!}{(n-k)!k!} p^k (1-p)^{n-k}$$

Here, $P(k;n,p)$ denotes the probability of having k heads in n trials. The mean of the binomial distribution is given by np and variance is given by $np(1-p)$. Have a look at the following graphs:

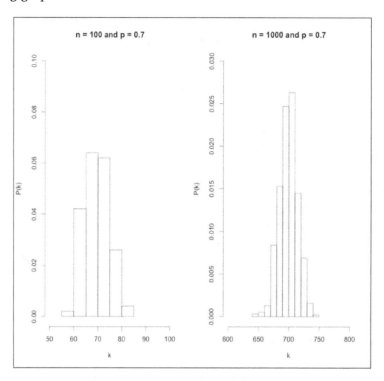

The preceding graphs show the binomial distribution for two values of n; 100 and 1000 for $p = 0.7$. As you can see, when n becomes large, the Binomial distribution becomes sharply peaked. It can be shown that, in the large n limit, a binomial distribution can be approximated using a normal distribution with mean np and variance $np(1-p)$. This is a characteristic shared by many discrete distributions that, in the large n limit, they can be approximated by some continuous distributions.

Beta distribution

The Beta distribution denoted by $Beta(x \mid \alpha, \beta)$ is a function of the power of x, and its reflection $(1-x)$ is given by:

$$Beta(x \mid \alpha, \beta) = \frac{1}{B(\alpha, \beta)} x^{\alpha-1} (1-x)^{\beta-1}$$

Here, $\alpha, \beta > 0$ are parameters that determine the shape of the distribution function and $B(\alpha, \beta)$ is the Beta function given by the ratio of Gamma functions: $B(\alpha, \beta) = \Gamma(\alpha)\Gamma(\beta)/\Gamma(\alpha + \beta)$.

The Beta distribution is a very important distribution in Bayesian inference. It is the conjugate prior probability distribution (which will be defined more precisely in the next chapter) for binomial, Bernoulli, negative binomial, and geometric distributions. It is used for modeling the random behavior of percentages and proportions. For example, the Beta distribution has been used for modeling **allele** frequencies in population genetics, time allocation in project management, the proportion of minerals in rocks, and heterogeneity in the probability of HIV transmission.

Gamma distribution

The Gamma distribution denoted by $Gamma(x \mid \alpha, \beta)$ is another common distribution used in Bayesian inference. It is used for modeling the waiting times such as survival rates. Special cases of the Gamma distribution are the well-known Exponential and Chi-Square distributions.

In Bayesian inference, the Gamma distribution is used as a conjugate prior for the inverse of variance of a one-dimensional normal distribution or parameters such as the rate (λ) of an exponential or Poisson distribution.

The mathematical form of a Gamma distribution is given by:

$$Gamma(x \mid \alpha, \beta) = \frac{\beta^{\alpha}}{\Gamma(\alpha)} x^{\alpha-1} exp(-x\beta)$$

Here, α and β are the shape and rate parameters, respectively (both take values greater than zero). There is also a form in terms of the scale parameter ($\theta = 1/\beta$), which is common in **econometrics**. Another related distribution is the Inverse-Gamma distribution that is the distribution of the reciprocal of a variable that is distributed according to the Gamma distribution. It's mainly used in Bayesian inference as the conjugate prior distribution for the variance of a one-dimensional normal distribution.

Dirichlet distribution

The Dirichlet distribution is a multivariate analogue of the Beta distribution. It is commonly used in Bayesian inference as the conjugate prior distribution for multinomial distribution and categorical distribution. The main reason for this is that it is easy to implement inference techniques, such as Gibbs sampling, on the Dirichlet-multinomial distribution.

The Dirichlet distribution of order K is defined over an open $(K-1)$ dimensional simplex as follows:

$$Dir(x \mid \infty) = \frac{1}{B(\infty)} \prod_{1}^{K} x_i^{\infty_i - 1}$$

Here, $x_1, x_2, \cdots, x_{K-1} > 0$, $x_1 + x_2 + \cdots + x_{K-1} < 1$, and $x_K = 1 - x_1 - \cdots - x_{K-1}$.

Wishart distribution

The Wishart distribution is a multivariate generalization of the Gamma distribution. It is defined over symmetric non-negative matrix-valued random variables. In Bayesian inference, it is used as the conjugate prior to estimate the distribution of inverse of the covariance matrix Σ^{-1} (or precision matrix) of the normal distribution. When we discussed Gamma distribution, we said it is used as a conjugate distribution for the inverse of the variance of the one-dimensional normal distribution.

The mathematical definition of the Wishart distribution is as follows:

$$W_p(X \mid V, n) = \frac{1}{2^{\frac{np}{2}} |V|^{\frac{n}{2}} \Gamma_p\left(\frac{n}{2}\right)} |X|^{\frac{n-p-1}{2}} exp\left(-\frac{1}{2} tr\left(V^{-1}X\right)\right)$$

Here, $|X|$ denotes the determinant of the matrix X of dimension $p \times p$ and $n \geq p$ is the degrees of freedom.

A special case of the Wishart distribution is when $p = V = 1$ corresponds to the well-known Chi-Square distribution function with n degrees of freedom.

Wikipedia gives a list of more than 100 useful distributions that are commonly used by statisticians (reference 1 in the *Reference* section of this chapter). Interested readers should refer to this article.

Exercises

1. By using the definition of conditional probability, show that any multivariate joint distribution of N random variables $[x_1, x_2, \cdots, x_N]$ has the following trivial factorization:

$$P(x_1, x_2, \cdots, x_N) = P(x_1 \mid x_2, \cdots, x_N) P(x_2 \mid x_3, \cdots, x_N) \cdots P(x_{N-1} \mid x_N) P(x_N)$$

2. The bivariate normal distribution is given by:

$$N(x \mid \mu, \Sigma) = \frac{1}{\sqrt{(2\pi)^N |\Sigma|}} exp\left(-\frac{1}{2}(x-\mu)^T \Sigma^{-1}(x-\mu)\right)$$

Here:

$$\mu = \begin{pmatrix} \mu_1 \\ \mu_2 \end{pmatrix}, \quad \Sigma = \begin{pmatrix} \sigma_1^2 & \rho\sigma_1\sigma_2 \\ \rho\sigma_2\sigma_1 & \sigma_2^2 \end{pmatrix}$$

By using the definition of conditional probability, show that the conditional distribution $P(x_1 \mid x_2)$ can be written as a normal distribution of the form $N(x_1 \mid \tilde{\mu}, \tilde{\sigma})$ where $\tilde{\mu} = \mu_1 + \rho\frac{\sigma_1}{\sigma_2}(x_2 - \mu_2)$ and $\tilde{\sigma} = (1 - u^2)\sigma_1^2$.

3. By using explicit integration of the expression in exercise 2, show that the marginalization of bivariate normal distribution will result in univariate normal distribution.

4. In the following table, a dataset containing the measurements of petal and sepal sizes of 15 different Iris flowers are shown (taken from the Iris dataset, UCI machine learning dataset repository). All units are in cms:

Sepal Length	Sepal Width	Petal Length	Petal Width	Class of Flower
5.1	3.5	1.4	0.2	Iris-setosa
4.9	3	1.4	0.2	Iris-setosa
4.7	3.2	1.3	0.2	Iris-setosa
4.6	3.1	1.5	0.2	Iris-setosa
5	3.6	1.4	0.2	Iris-setosa
7	3.2	4.7	1.4	Iris-versicolor

Sepal Length	Sepal Width	Petal Length	Petal Width	Class of Flower
6.4	3.2	4.5	1.5	Iris-versicolor
6.9	3.1	4.9	1.5	Iris-versicolor
5.5	2.3	4	1.3	Iris-versicolor
6.5	2.8	4.6	1.5	Iris-versicolor
6.3	3.3	6	2.5	Iris-virginica
5.8	2.7	5.1	1.9	Iris-virginica
7.1	3	5.9	2.1	Iris-virginica
6.3	2.9	5.6	1.8	Iris-virginica
6.5	3	5.8	2.2	Iris-virginica

Answer the following questions:

1. What is the probability of finding flowers with a sepal length more than 5 cm and a sepal width less than 3 cm?

2. What is the probability of finding flowers with a petal length less than 1.5 cm; given that petal width is equal to 0.2 cm?

3. What is the probability of finding flowers with a sepal length less than 6 cm and a petal width less than 1.5 cm; given that the class of the flower is Iris-versicolor?

References

1. http://en.wikipedia.org/wiki/List_of_probability_distributions

2. Feller W. *An Introduction to Probability Theory and Its Applications.*
Vol. 1. Wiley Series in Probability and Mathematical Statistics. 1968.
ISBN-10: 0471257087

3. Jayes E.T. *Probability Theory: The Logic of Science.* Cambridge University Press.
2003. ISBN-10: 0521592712

4. Radziwill N.M. *Statistics (The Easier Way) with R: an informal text on applied statistics.* Lapis Lucera. 2015. ISBN-10: 0692339426

Summary

To summarize this chapter, we discussed elements of probability theory; particularly those aspects required for learning Bayesian inference. Due to lack of space, we have not covered many elementary aspects of this subject. There are some excellent books on this subject, for example, books by William Feller (reference 2 in the *References* section of this chapter), E. T. Jaynes (reference 3 in the *References* section of this chapter), and M. Radziwill (reference 4 in the *References* section of this chapter). Readers are encouraged to read these to get a more in-depth understanding of probability theory and how it can be applied in real-life situations.

In the next chapter, we will introduce the R programming language that is the most popular open source framework for data analysis and Bayesian inference in particular.

2
The R Environment

R is currently one of the most popular programming environments for statistical computing. It was evolved as an open source language from the S programming language developed at Bell Labs. The main creators of R are two academicians, Robert Gentleman and Ross Ihaka, from the University of Auckland in New Zealand.

The main reasons for the popularity of R, apart from free software under GNU General Public License, are the following:

- R is very easy to use. It is an interpreted language and at the same time can be used for procedural programming.

- R supports both functional and object-oriented paradigms. It has very strong graphical and data visualization capabilities.

- Through its LaTex-like documentation support, R can be used for making high-quality documentation.

- Being an open source software, R has a large number of contributed packages that makes almost all statistical modeling possible in this environment.

This chapter is intended to give a basic introduction to R so that any reader who is not familiar with the language can follow the rest of the book by reading through this chapter. It is not possible to give a detailed description of the R language in one chapter and the interested reader should consult books specially written in R programming. I would recommend *The Art of R Programming* (reference 1 in the *References* section of this chapter) and *R Cookbook* (reference 2 in the *References* section of this chapter) for those users who are mainly interested in using R for analyzing and modeling data. For those who are interested in learning about the advanced features of R, for example, for writing complex programs or R packages, *Advanced R* (reference 3 in the *References* section of this chapter) is an excellent book.

Setting up the R environment and packages

R is a free software under GNU open source license. R comes with a basic package and also has a large number of user-contributed packages for advanced analysis and modeling. It also has a nice graphics user interface-based editor called RStudio. In this section, we will learn how to download R, set up the R environment in your computer, and write a simple R program.

Installing R and RStudio

The Comprehensive R Archive Network (CRAN) hosts all releases of R and the contributed packages. R for Windows can be installed by downloading the binary of the base package from `http://cran.r-project.org`; a standard installation should be sufficient. For Linux and Mac OS X, the webpage gives instructions on how to download and install the software. At the time of writing this book, the latest release was version 3.1.2. Various packages need to be installed separately from the package page. One can install any package from the R command prompt using the following command:

```
install.packages("package name")
```

After installing the package, one needs to load the package before using it with the following command:

```
library("package name")
```

A very useful **integrated development environment (IDE)** for R is RStudio. It can be downloaded freely from `http://www.rstudio.com/`. RStudio works on Windows, Linux, and Mac platforms. It has both a desktop version and also a server version that can be used for writing R programs through a browser interface on a remote server. After installing R and RStudio, it is useful to set the default working directory to the directory of your choice. RStudio reads and writes files containing R codes into the working directory. To find out what the current directory is, use the R command `getwd( )`. To change the working directory to a directory of your preference, use the following command:

```
setwd("directory path")
```

You can also set this from the menu bar of RStudio by clicking on **Session | Set Working Directory**.

Your first R program

Let us write a simple program to add two integers x and y resulting in their sum z. On the command prompt in RStudio, type the following commands and press *Enter*:

```
>x <-2
>y <-3
>z <-x+y
>print(z)
[1]   5
```

Now, you can assign different values to x and y and print z to see how z changes. Instead of print(z), you can also simply enter z to print its values.

Managing data in R

Before we start any serious programming in R, we need to learn how to import data into an R environment and which data types R supports. Often, for a particular analysis, we will not use the entire dataset. Therefore, we need to also learn how to select a subset of the data for any analysis. This section will cover these aspects.

Data Types in R

R has five basic data types as follows:

- Integer
- Numeric (real)
- Complex
- Character
- Logical (True/False)

The default representation of numbers in R is double precision real number (numeric). If you want an integer representation explicitly, you need to add the suffix L. For example, simply entering 1 on the command prompt will store 1 as a numeric object. To store 1 as an integer, you need to enter 1L. The command class(x) will give the class (type) of the object x. Therefore, entering class(1) on command prompt will give the answer numeric whereas entering class(1L) will give the answer integer.

R also has a special number Inf that represents Infinity. The number NaN (*not a number*) is used to represent an undefined value such as 0/0. Missing values are represented by using the symbol NA.

Data structures in R

The data structures in R can be classified as either homogeneous (all elements containing the same data type) or heterogeneous (elements containing different data types). Furthermore, each of these have different structures depending upon the number of dimensions:

- Homogeneous:
  - **Atomic vector**: one-dimensional
  - **Matrix**: two-dimensional
  - **Array**: N-dimensional

- Heterogeneous:
  - **List**: one-dimensional
  - **Data frame**: two-dimensional

The most basic object in R is a vector. To create an empty integer vector of size 10, enter the following command on the R prompt:

```
>v <-vector("integer",10)
>v
[1]  0000000000
```

You can assign the value *m* to *n*th component of the vector using the following command:

```
> v[5] <-1
> v
[1]  0000100000
```

Readers should note that unlike in many programming languages, the array index in R starts with 1 and not 0.

Whereas a vector can only contain objects of the same type, a list, although similar to the vector, can contain objects of different types. The following command will create a list containing integers, real numbers, and characters:

```
> l <-list(1L, 2L, 3, 4, "a", "b")
> str(l)
List of 6
$: int 1
$: int 2
$: num 3
$: num 4
$: chr "a"
$: chr "b"
```

Here, we used the `str()` function in R that shows the structure of any R object.

R has a special function `c()` to combine multiple numbers of basic data into a vector or list. For example, `c(1,3,6,2,-1)` will produce a vector containing numbers from 1,2,3,6,-1:

```
> c(1, 3, 6, 2, -1)
[1]  1 3 6 2 -1
```

A matrix is the generalization of a vector into two dimensions. Consider the following command:

```
>m <-matrix(c(1:9),nrow=3,ncol=3)
```

This command will generate a matrix m of size 3 x 3 containing numbers from 1 to 9.

The most common data structure used for storing data in R is a data frame. A data frame, like the list, can contain data of different types (numeric, integer, Boolean, or character). It is essentially a list of vectors of equal length. Therefore, it has the same two-dimensional structure as a matrix. The length (found using `length( )`) of a data frame is the length of the underlying list that is the number of columns in the data frame. There are simple commands `nrow( )` and `ncol( )` for finding the number of rows and columns of a data frame. The other two attributes of a data frame are `rownames( )` and `colnames( )` that can be used to either set or find the names of rows or columns.

Importing data into R

Data that is in the form of a table can be easily loaded into R using the read.table(...) function. It has several arguments to make the import very flexible. Some of the useful arguments are the following:

- file: The name of a file or a complete URL
- header: A logical value indicating whether the file has a header line containing names of the variables
- sep: A character indicating the column separator field
- row.names: A vector of row names
- col.names: A vector of names for variables
- skip: The number of lines in the data file to be skipped before reading the data
- nrows: The number of rows in the dataset
- stringsASFactors: A logical value indicating if the character variables can be coded as factors or not

For small datasets, one can use read.table("filename.txt") without specifying other arguments; the rest R will figure out itself. Another useful function is read.csv() for reading CSV files only.

In addition to loading data from text files, data can be imported into R by connecting to external databases through various interfaces. One such popular interface is **Open Database Connectivity (ODBC)**. The **RODBC** package in R provides access to different databases through the ODBC interface. This package contains different functions for connecting with a database and performing various operations. Some of the important functions in the RODBC package are as follows:

- odbcConnect(dsn, uid="user_name", pwd="password"): Used to open a connection to an ODBC database having registered data source name dsn.
- sqlFetch(channel, sqtable): Used to read a table from an ODBC database to a data frame.
- sqlQuery(channel, query): Used to submit a query to an ODBC database and return the results.
- sqlSave(channel, mydf, tablename = sqtable, append = FALSE): Used to write or update (append = TRUE) a data frame to a table in the ODBC database.
- close(channel): Used to close the connection. Here, channel is the connection handle as returned by odbcConnect.

Slicing and dicing datasets

Often, in data analysis, one needs to slice and dice the full data frame to select a few variables or observations. This is called subsetting. R has some powerful and fast methods for doing this.

To extract subsets of R objects, one can use the following three operators:

- **Single bracket [ ]**: This returns an object of the same class as the original. The single bracket operator can be used to select more than one element of an object. Some examples are as follows:

```
>x <-c(10,20,30,40,50)
>x[1:3]
[1]   10 20 30

>x[x >25]
[1]   30 40 50

>f <-x >30
>x[f]
[1]   40 50

>m <-matrix(c(1:9),nrow=3,ncol=3)
>m[1 ,] #select the entire first row
[1]   1 4 7

>m[ ,2] #select the entire second column
[1]   4 5 6
```

- **Double bracket [[ ]]**: This is used to extract a single element of a list or data frame. The returned object need not be the same type as the initial object. Some examples are as follows:

```
>y <-list("a", "b", "c", "d", "e")

>y[1]
[[1]]
[1]   "a"

>class(y[1])
[1]   "list"

>y[[1]]
[1]   "a"

>class(y[[1]])
[1]   "character"
```

- **Dollar sign $**: This is used to extract elements of a list or data frame by name. Some examples are as follows:

```
>z <-list(John = 12 ,Mary = 18,Alice = 24 ,Bob = 17 ,Tom = 21)

>z$Bob
[1] 17
```

- **Use of negative index values**: This is used to drop a particular index or column—one subset with a negative sign for the corresponding index. For example, to drop Mary and Bob from the preceding list, use the following code:

```
> y <-z[c(-2, -4)]
> y
```

Vectorized operations

In R, many operations, such as arithmetical operations involving vectors and matrices, can be done very efficiently using vectorized operations. For example, if you are adding two vectors x and y, their elements are added in parallel. This also makes the code more concise and easier to understand. For example, one does not need a `for( )` loop to add two vectors in the code:

```
>x <-c(1,2,3,4,5)

>y <-c(10,20,30,40,50)

>z <-x+y

>z
[1]    11 22 33 44 55

>w <-x*y

>w
[1]    10 40 90 160 250
```

Another very useful example of vectorized operations is in the case of matrices. If X and Y are two matrices, the following operations can be carried out in R in a vectorized form:

```
>X*Y  ## Element-wise multiplication
>X/Y  ## Element-wise division
>X  %*%  Y  ## Standard matrix multiplication
```

Writing R programs

Although much data analysis in R can be carried out in an interactive manner using command prompt, often for more complex tasks, one needs to write R scripts. As mentioned in the introduction, R has both the perspective of a functional and object-oriented programming language. In this section, some of the standard syntaxes of the programming in R are described.

Control structures

Control structures are meant for controlling the flow of execution of a program. The standard control structures are as follows:

- `if` and `else`: To test a condition
- `for`: To loop over a set of statements for a fixed number of times
- `while`: To loop over a set of statements while a condition is true
- `repeat`: To execute an infinite loop
- `break`: To break the execution of a loop
- `next`: To skip an iteration of a loop
- `return`: To exit a function

Functions

If one wants to use R for more serious programming, it is essential to know how to write functions. They make the language more powerful and elegant. R has many built-in functions, such as `mean()`, `sort()`, `sin()`, `plot()`, and many more, which are written using R commands.

A function is defined as follows:

```
>fname<-function(arg1,arg2,    ){
        R Expressions
    }
```

Here, `fname` is the name of the function; `arg1`, `arg2`, and so on, are arguments passed to the function. Note that unlike in other languages, functions in R do not end with a return statement. By default, the last statement executed inside the body of the function is returned by the function.

Once a function is defined, it is executed simply by entering the function name with the values for the arguments:

```
>fname(arg1,arg2,…)
```

The important properties of functions in R are as follows:

- Functions are first-class citizens
- Functions can be passed as arguments to other functions
- One can define a function inside another function (nesting)
- The arguments of the functions can be matched by position or name

Let's consider a simple example of a function, which given an input vector x, calculates its mean. To write this function, open a new window in RStudio for R script from the menu bar through **File | New File | R Script**. In this R script, enter the following lines of code:

```
myMean <-function(x){
    s <-sum(x)
    l <-length(x)
    mean <-s/l
    mean
}
```

Select the entire code and use the keys *Ctrl + Enter* to execute the script. This completes the definition of the myMean function. To use this function on the command prompt, enter the following:

```
>x <-c(10,20,30,40,50)
>myMean(x)
```

This will generate the following result:

```
>myMean(x)
[1]   30
```

Scoping rules

In programming languages, it is very important to understand the scopes of all variables to avoid errors during execution. There are two types of scoping of a variable in a function: lexical scoping and dynamic scoping. In the case of lexical scoping, the value of a variable in a function is looked up in the environment in which the function was defined. Generally, this is the global environment. In the case of dynamic scoping, the value of a variable is looked up in the environment in which the function was called (the calling environment).

R uses lexical scoping that makes it possible to write functions inside a function. This is illustrated with the following example:

```
>x <-0.1
>f <-function(y){
        x*y
    }
>g <-function(y){
        x<-5
        x-f(y)
    }
>g(10)
[1]   4
```

The answer is 4 because while evaluating function f, the value of x is taken from the global environment, which is 0.1, whereas while evaluating function g, the value of x is taken from the local environment of g, which is 5.

Lexical scoping has some disadvantages. Since the value of a variable is looked up from the environment in which the function is defined, all functions must carry a pointer to their respective defining environments. Also, all objects must be stored in memory during the execution of the program.

Loop functions

Often, we have a list containing some objects and we want to apply a function to every element of the list. For example, we have a list of results of a survey, containing *m* questions from *n* participants. We would like to find the average response for each question (assuming that all questions have a response as numeric values). One could use a for loop over the set of questions and find an average among *n* users using the mean() function in R. Loop functions come in handy in such situations and one can do such computations in a more compact way. These are like iterators in other languages such as Java.

The following are the standard loop functions in R:

- lapply: To loop over a list and evaluate a function on each element
- sapply: The same as lapply, but with the output in a more simpler form
- mapply: A multivariate version of sapply
- apply: To apply functions over array margins
- tapply: To apply a function to each cell of a ragged array

lapply

The `lapply()` function is used in the following manner:

```
>lapply(X,FUN,    )
```

Here, X is a list or vector containing data. The FUN is the name of a function that needs to be applied on each element of the list or vector. The last argument represents optional arguments. The result of using `lapply` is always a list, regardless of the type of input.

As an example, consider the quarterly revenue of four companies in billions of dollars (not real data). We would like to compute the yearly average revenue of all four companies as follows:

```
>X<-list(HP=c(12.5,14.3,16.1,15.4),IBM=c(22,24.5,23.7,26.2),Dell=c(8.9
,9.7,10.8,11.5),Oracle=c(20.5,22.7,21.8,24.4)   )
>lapply(X,mean)
$HP
[1]   14.575

$IBM
[1]   24.1

$Dell
[1]   10.225

$Oracle
[1]   22.35
```

sapply

The `sapply()` function is similar to `lapply()` with the additional option of simplifying the output into a desired form. For example, `sapply()` can be used in the previous dataset as follows:

```
> sapply(X,mean,simplify="array")
    HP       IBM       Dell      Oracle
   14.575    24.100    10.225    22.350
```

mapply

The `lapply()` and `sapply()` functions can only have one argument. If you want to apply a function with multiple variable arguments, then `mapply()` becomes handy. Here is how it is used:

```
>mapply(FUN,L₁,L₂,    ,Lₙ,SIMPLIFY=TRUE)
```

Here, $L_1, L_2, \cdots, L_n$ are the lists to which the function FUN needs to be applied. For example, consider the following list generation command:

```
>rep(x=10,times=5)
[1] 10 10 10 10 10
```

Here, the `rep` function repeats the value of x five times. Suppose we want to create a list where the number 10 occurs 1 time, the number 20 occurs 2 times, and so on, we can use `mapply` as follows:

```
>mapply(rep,x=c(10,20,30,40,50),times=1:5)
```

apply

The `apply()` function is useful for applying a function to the margins of an array or matrix. The form of the function is as follows:

```
>apply(X,MARGIN,FUN,    )
```

Here, MARGIN is a vector giving the subscripts that the function will be applied over. For example, in the case of a matrix, 1 indicates rows and 2 indicates columns, and `c(1,2)` indicates rows and columns. Consider the following example as an illustration:

```
>Y <-matrix(1:9,nrow=3,ncol=3)
>Y
          [,1]          [,2]          [,3]
[1,]         1            4            7
[2,]         2            5            8
[1,]         3            6            9
>apply(Y,1,sum) #sum along the row
[1]   12 15 18
>apply(Y,2,sum) #sum along the column
[1]    6 15 24
```

tapply

The `tapply()` function is used to apply a function over the subsets of a vector. The function description is as follows:

```
>tapply(X,INDEX,FUN,SIMPLIFY=TRUE)
```

Let us consider the earlier example of the quarterly revenue of five companies:

```
>X<-X(HP=c(12.5,14.3,16.1,15.4),IBM=c(22,24.5,23.7,26.2),Dell=c(8.9,9.
7,10.8,11.5),Oracle=c(20.5,22.7,21.8,24.4)  )
```

Using `lapply()`, we found the average yearly revenue of each company. Suppose we want to find the revenue per quarter averaged over all four companies, we can use `tapply()` as follows; here we use the function c instead of the list to create X:

```
>X<-c(HP=c(12.5,14.3,16.1,15.4),IBM=c(22,24.5,23.7,26.2),Dell
    =c(8.9,9.7,10.8,11.5),Oracle=c(20.5,22.7,21.8,24.4)  )

>f<-factor(rep(c("Q1","Q2","Q3","Q4"),times=4)  )
>f
[1]   Q1 Q2 Q3 Q4 Q1 Q2 Q3 Q4 Q1 Q2 Q3 Q4 Q1 Q2 Q3 Q4
Levels Q1 Q2 Q3 Q4

>tapply(X,f,mean,simplify=TRUE)
Q1              Q2              Q3              Q4
15.97           17.80           18.10           19.37
```

By creating the factor list with levels as quarter values, we can apply the mean function for each quarter using `tapply()`.

Data visualization

One of the powerful features of R is its functions for generating high-quality plots and visualize data. The graphics functions in R can be divided into three groups:

- High-level plotting functions to create new plots, add axes, labels, and titles.
- Low-level plotting functions to add more information to an existing plot. This includes adding extra points, lines, and labels.
- Interactive graphics functions to interactively add information to, or extract information from, an existing plot.

The R base package itself contains several graphics functions. For more advanced graph applications, one can use packages such as **ggplot2**, **grid**, or **lattice**. In particular, ggplot2 is very useful for generating visually appealing, multilayered graphs. It is based on the concept of *grammar of graphics*. Due to lack of space, we are not covering these packages in this book. Interested readers should consult the book by Hadley Wickham (reference 4 in the *References* section of this chapter).

High-level plotting functions

Let us start with the most basic plotting functions in R as follows:

- `plot( )`: This is the most common plotting function in R. It is a generic function where the output depends on the type of the first argument.
- `plot(x, y)`: This produces a scatter plot of y versus x.
- `plot(x)`: If x is a real value vector, the output will be a plot of the value of x versus its index on the X axis. If x is a complex number, then it will plot the real part versus the imaginary part.
- `plot(f, y)`: Here, f is a factor object and y is a numeric vector. The function produces box plots of y for each level of f.
- `plot(y ~ expr)`: Here, y is any object and expr is a list of object names separated by + (for example, $p + q + r$). The function plots y against every object named in expr.

There are two useful functions in R for visualizing multivariate data:

- `pairs(X)`: If X is a data frame containing numeric data, then this function produces a pair-wise scatter plot matrix of the variables defined by the columns of X.
- `coplot(y ~ x | z)`: If y and x are numeric vectors and z is a factor object, then this function plots y versus x for every level of z.

For plotting distributions of data, one can use the following functions:

- `hist(x)`: This produces a histogram of the numeric vector x.
- `qqplot(x, y)`: This plots the quantiles of x versus the quantiles of y to compare their respective distributions.
- `qqnorm(x)`: This plots the numeric vector x against the expected normal order scores.

Low-level plotting commands

To add points and lines to a plot, the following commands can be used:

- `points(x, y)`: This adds point (x, y) to the current plot.
- `lines(x, y)`: This adds a connecting line to the current plot.
- `abline(a, b)`: This adds a line of the slope `b` and intercepts `a` to the current plot.
- `polygon(x, y, ...)`: This draws a polygon defined by the ordered vertices (x, y, …).

To add the text to a plot, use the following functions:

- `text(x, y, labels)`: This adds text to the current plot at point (x, y).
- `legend(x, y, legend)`: This adds a legend to the current plot at point (x, y).
- `title(main, sub)`: This adds a title `main` at the top of the current plot in a large font and a subtitle `sub` at the bottom in a smaller font.
- `axis(side, ...)`: This adds an axis to the current plot on the side given by the first argument. The `side` can take values from 1 to 4 counting clockwise from the bottom.

The following example shows how to plot a scatter plot and add a trend line. For this, we will use the famous Iris dataset, created by R. A. Fisher, that is available in R itself:

```
data(iris)
str(iris)
plot(iris$Petal.Width, iris$Petal.Length, col = "blue", xlab = "X",
ylab = "Y")
title(main = "Plot of Iris Data", sub = "Petal Length (Y) Vs Petal
Width (X)")
fitlm <- lm(iris$Petal.Length ~ iris$Petal.Width)
abline(fitlm[1], fitlm[2], col = "red")
```

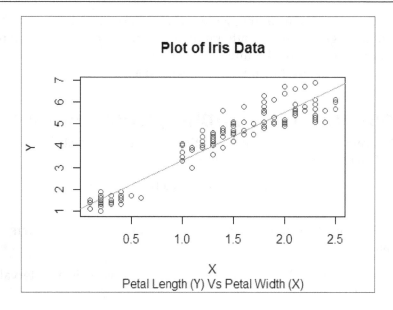

Interactive graphics functions

There are functions in R that enable users to add or extract information from a plot using the mouse in an interactive manner:

- `locator (n , type)`: This waits for the user to select the n locations on the current plot using the left-mouse button. Here, type is one of n, p, l or o to plot points or lines at these locations. For example, to place a legend *Outlier* near an outlier point, use the following code:

```
>text(locator(1),"Outlier" ,adj=0")
```

- `identify(x, y, label)`: This allows the user to highlight any of the points, x and y, selected using the left-mouse button by placing the label nearby.

Sampling

Often, we would be interested in creating a representative dataset, for some analysis or design of experiments, by sampling from a population. This is particularly the case for Bayesian inference, as we will see in the later chapters, where samples are drawn from posterior distribution for inference. Therefore, it would be useful to learn how to sample N points from some well-known distributions in this chapter.

Before we use any particular sampling methods, readers should note that R, like any other computer program, uses pseudo random number generators for sampling. It is useful to supply a starting seed number to get reproducible results. This can be done using the set.seed(n) command with an integer n as the seed.

Random uniform sampling from an interval

To generate *n* random numbers (numeric) that are uniformly distributed in the interval *[a, b]*, one can use the runif() function:

```
>runif(5,1,10)   #generates 5 random numbers between 1 and 10
[1]   7.416    9.846    3.093    2.656    1.561
```

Without any arguments, runif() will generate uniform random numbers between 0 and 1.

If we want to generate random integers uniformly distributed in an interval, the function to use is sample():

```
>sample(1:100,10,replace=T)    #generates 10 random integers
                                        between 1 and 100
[1]   24 51 46 87 30 86 50 45 53 62
```

The option replace=T indicates that the repetition is allowed.

Sampling from normal distribution

Often, we may want to generate data that is distributed according to a particular distribution, say normal distribution. In the case of univariate distributions, R has several in-built functions for this. For sampling data from a normal distribution, the function to be used is rnorm(). For example, consider the following code:

```
>rnorm(5,mean=0,sd=1)
[1]   0.759  -1.676   0.569  0.928 -0.609
```

This generates five random numbers distributed according to a normal distribution with mean 0 and standard deviation 1.

Similarly, one can use the rbinom() function for sampling from a binomial distribution, rpois() to sample from a Poisson distribution, rbeta() to sample from a Beta distribution, and rgamma() to sample from a Gamma distribution to mention a few other distributions.

Exercises

For the following exercises in this chapter, we use the Auto MPG dataset from the UCI Machine Learning repository (references 5 and 6 in the *References* section of this chapter). The dataset can be downloaded from `https://archive.ics.uci.edu/ml/datasets.html`. The dataset contains the fuel consumption of cars in the US measured during 1970-1982. Along with consumption values, there are attribute variables, such as the number of cylinders, displacement, horse power, weight, acceleration, year, origin, and the name of the car:

- Load the dataset into R using the `read.table()` function.
- Produce a box plot of mpg values for each car name.
- Write a function that will compute the scaled value (subtract the mean and divide by standard deviation) of a column whose name is given as an argument of the function.
- Use the `lapply()` function to compute scaled values for all variables.
- Produce a scatter plot of mgp versus acceleration for each car name using `coplot()`. Use legends to annotate the graph.

References

1. Matloff N. *The Art of R Programming – A Tour of Statistical Software Design*. No Starch Press. 2011. ISBN-10: 1593273843

2. Teetor P. *R Cookbook*. O'Reilly Media. 2011. ISBN-10: 0596809158

3. Wickham H. *Advanced R*. Chapman & Hall/CRC The R Series. 2015. ISBN-10: 1466586966

4. Wickham H. *ggplot2: Elegant Graphics for Data Analysis (Use R!)*. Springer. 2010. ISBN-10: 0387981403

5. Auto MPG Data Set, UCI Machine Learning repository, `https://archive.ics.uci.edu/ml/datasets/Auto+MPG`

6. Quinlan R. "Combining Instance-Based and Model-Based Learning". In: Tenth International Conference of Machine Learning. 236-243. University of Massachusetts, Amherst. Morgan Kaufmann. 1993

Downloading the example code

You can download the example code files from your account at
`http://www.packtpub.com` for all the Packt Publishing books
you have purchased. If you purchased this book elsewhere, you can
visit `http://www.packtpub.com/support` and register to have
the files e-mailed directly to you.

Summary

In this chapter, you were introduced to the R environment. After reading through
this chapter, you learned how to import data into R, make a selection of subsets of
data for their analysis, and write simple R programs using functions and control
structures. Also, you should now be familiar with the graphical capabilities of R
and some advanced capabilities, such as loop functions. In the next chapter, we
will begin the central theme of this book, Bayesian inference.

3
Introducing Bayesian Inference

In *Chapter 1*, *Introducing the Probability Theory*, we learned about the Bayes theorem as the relation between conditional probabilities of two random variables such as *A* and *B*. This theorem is the basis for updating beliefs or model parameter values in Bayesian inference, given the observations. In this chapter, a more formal treatment of Bayesian inference will be given. To begin with, let us try to understand how uncertainties in a real-world problem are treated in Bayesian approach.

Bayesian view of uncertainty

The classical or frequentist statistics typically take the view that any physical process-generating data containing noise can be modeled by a stochastic model with fixed values of parameters. The parameter values are learned from the observed data through procedures such as **maximum likelihood estimate**. The essential idea is to search in the parameter space to find the parameter values that maximize the probability of observing the data seen so far. Neither the uncertainty in the estimation of model parameters from data, nor the uncertainty in the model itself that explains the phenomena under study, is dealt with in a formal way. *The Bayesian approach, on the other hand, treats all sources of uncertainty using probabilities*. Therefore, neither the model to explain an observed dataset nor its parameters are fixed, but they are treated as uncertain variables. Bayesian inference provides a framework to learn the entire distribution of model parameters, not just the values, which maximize the probability of observing the given data. The learning can come from both the evidence provided by observed data and domain knowledge from experts. There is also a framework to select the best model among the family of models suited to explain a given dataset.

Once we have the distribution of model parameters, we can eliminate the effect of uncertainty of parameter estimation in the future values of a random variable predicted using the learned model. This is done by averaging over the model parameter values through marginalization of joint probability distribution, as explained in *Chapter 1, Introducing the Probability Theory*.

Consider the joint probability distribution of N random variables again, as discussed in *Chapter 1, Introducing the Probability Theory*:

$$P\left(x_1, x_2, \cdots, x_N \mid \boldsymbol{\theta}, m\right)$$

This time, we have added one more term, m, to the argument of the probability distribution, in order to indicate explicitly that the parameters $\boldsymbol{\theta}$ are generated by the model m. Then, according to Bayes theorem, the probability distribution of model parameters conditioned on the observed data $X = \{x_1, x_2, \cdots, x_N\}$ and model m is given by:

$$P\left(\boldsymbol{\theta} \mid x_1, x_2, \cdots, x_N, m\right) = \frac{P\left(x_1, x_2, \cdots, x_N \mid \boldsymbol{\theta}, m\right) P\left(\boldsymbol{\theta} \mid m\right)}{P\left(x_1, x_2, \cdots, x_N \mid m\right)}$$

Formally, the term on the LHS of the equation $P(\boldsymbol{\theta} \mid x_1, x_2, \cdots, x_N, m)$ is called **posterior probability distribution**. The second term appearing in the numerator of RHS, $P(\boldsymbol{\theta} \mid m)$, is called the **prior probability distribution**. It represents the prior belief about the model parameters, before observing any data, say, from the domain knowledge. Prior distributions can also have parameters and they are called hyperparameters. The term $P(x_1, x_2, \cdots, x_N \mid \boldsymbol{\theta}, m)$ is the likelihood of model m explaining the observed data. Since $P(x_1, x_2, \cdots, x_N \mid m) = \int P(x_1, x_2, \cdots, x_N \mid \boldsymbol{\theta}, m) P(\boldsymbol{\theta} \mid m) d\theta$, it can be considered as a normalization constant Z_N. The preceding equation can be rewritten in an iterative form as follows:

$$P\left(\boldsymbol{\theta}^n \mid X^n, m\right) = \frac{1}{Z_N^{\,n}} P\left(X^n \mid \boldsymbol{\theta}^{n-1}, m\right) P\left(\boldsymbol{\theta}^{n-1} \mid m\right)$$

Here, $X^n = \{x_1^n, x_2^n, \cdots, x_N^n\}$ represents values of observations that are obtained at time step n, $P(\theta^{n-1} \mid m)$ is the marginal parameter distribution updated until time step $n - 1$, and $P(\theta^n \mid X^n, m)$ is the model parameter distribution updated after seeing the observations X^n at time step n.

Casting Bayes theorem in this iterative form is useful for online learning and it suggests the following:

- Model parameters can be learned in an iterative way as more and more data or evidence is obtained
- The posterior distribution estimated using the data seen so far can be treated as a prior model when the next set of observations is obtained
- Even if no data is available, one could make predictions based on prior distribution created using the domain knowledge alone

To make these points clear, let's take a simple illustrative example. Consider the case where one is trying to estimate the distribution of the height of males in a given region. The data used for this example is the height measurement in centimeters obtained from M volunteers sampled randomly from the population. We assume that the heights are distributed according to a normal distribution with the mean μ and variance σ^2:

$$\{h_1, h_2, \cdots, h_M\} \sim N\left(h \mid \mu, \sigma^2\right)$$

As mentioned earlier, in classical statistics, one tries to estimate the values of μ and σ^2 from observed data. Apart from the best estimate value for each parameter, one could also determine an error term of the estimate. In the Bayesian approach, on the other hand, μ and σ^2 are also treated as random variables. Let's, for simplicity, assume σ^2 is a known constant. Also, let's assume that the prior distribution for μ is a normal distribution with (hyper) parameters μ^0 and $\left(\sigma^0\right)^2 = \tilde{\sigma}^2$. In this case, the expression for posterior distribution of μ is given by:

$$P\left(\mu \mid h_{1:M}, \sigma^2\right) = \frac{1}{Z}\left[\prod_{i=1}^{M} \frac{1}{\sqrt{2\sigma^2}} \exp\left\{-\frac{1}{2\sigma^2}\left(h_i - \mu\right)^2\right\}\right] \frac{1}{\sqrt{2\tilde{\sigma}^2}} \exp\left\{-\frac{1}{2\tilde{\sigma}^2}\left(\mu - \mu^0\right)^2\right\}$$

Here, for convenience, we have used the notation $h_{1:M}$ for $\{h_1, h_2, \cdots, h_M\}$. It is a simple exercise to expand the terms in the product and complete the squares in the exponential. This is given as an exercise at the end of the chapter. The resulting expression for the posterior distribution $P\left(\mu \mid h_{1:M}, \sigma^2\right)$ is given by:

$$P\left(\mu \mid h_{1:M}, \sigma^2\right) = \frac{1}{2}\exp\left\{-\frac{1}{2}\left(\frac{\tilde{\sigma}^2 + \sigma^2/M}{\tilde{\sigma}^2 \sigma^2/M}\right)\left[\mu - \left(\frac{\tilde{\sigma}^2}{\tilde{\sigma}^2 + \sigma^2/M}\bar{h} + \frac{\sigma^2/M}{\tilde{\sigma}^2 + \sigma^2/M}\mu^0\right)\right]^2\right\}$$

Here, $\bar{h} = \sum_{i=1}^{M} h_i / M$ represents the sample mean. Though the preceding expression looks complex, it has a very simple interpretation. The posterior distribution is also a normal distribution with the following mean:

$$\mu^M = \left(\frac{\tilde{\sigma}^2}{\tilde{\sigma}^2 + \sigma^2/M} \bar{h} + \frac{\sigma^2/M}{\tilde{\sigma}^2 + \sigma^2/M} \mu^0 \right)$$

The variance is as follows:

$$\left(\sigma^M \right)^2 = \frac{\tilde{\sigma}^2 \sigma^2 / M}{\tilde{\sigma}^2 + \sigma^2/M}$$

The posterior mean is a weighted sum of prior mean μ^0 *and sample mean* $\bar{h}$. As the sample size M increases, the weight of the sample mean increases and that of the prior decreases. Similarly, posterior precision (inverse of the variance) is the sum of the prior precision $\frac{1}{\tilde{\sigma}^2}$ and precision of the sample mean $\frac{M}{\sigma^2}$:

$$\frac{1}{\left(\sigma^M \right)^2} = \frac{M}{\sigma^2} + \frac{1}{\tilde{\sigma}^2}$$

As M increases, the contribution of precision from observations (evidence) outweighs that from the prior knowledge.

Let's take a concrete example where we consider age distribution with the population mean 5.5 and population standard deviation 0.5. We sample 100 people from this population by using the following R script:

```
>set.seed(100)
>age_samples <- rnorm(10000,mean = 5.5,sd=0.5)
```

We can calculate the posterior distribution using the following R function:

```
>age_mean <- function(n){
  mu0 <- 5
  sd0 <- 1
  mus <- mean(age_samples[1:n])
  sds <- sd(age_samples[1:n])
```

```
  mu_n <- (sd0^2/(sd0^2 + sds^2/n)) * mus + (sds^2/n/(sd0^2 +
sds^2/n)) * mu0
  mu_n
}
>samp <- c(25,50,100,200,400,500,1000,2000,5000,10000)
>mu <- sapply(samp,age_mean,simplify = "array")
>plot(samp,mu,type="b",col="blue",ylim=c(5.3,5.7),xlab="no of
samples",ylab="estimate of mean")
>abline(5.5,0)
```

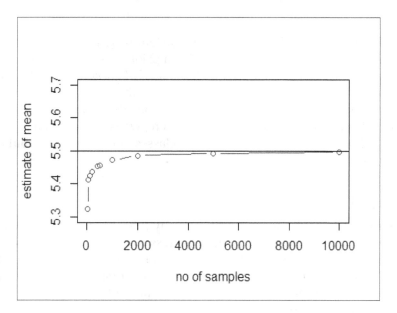

One can see that as the number of samples increases, the estimated mean asymptotically approaches the population mean. The initial low value is due to the influence of the prior, which is, in this case, 5.0.

This simple and intuitive picture of how the prior knowledge and evidence from observations contribute to the overall model parameter estimate holds in any Bayesian inference. The precise mathematical expression for how they combine would be different. Therefore, one could start using a model for prediction with just prior information, either from the domain knowledge or the data collected in the past. Also, as new observations arrive, the model can be updated using the Bayesian scheme.

Choosing the right prior distribution

In the preceding simple example, we saw that if the likelihood function has the form of a normal distribution, and when the prior distribution is chosen as normal, the posterior also turns out to be a normal distribution. Also, we could get a closed-form analytical expression for the posterior mean. Since the posterior is obtained by multiplying the prior and likelihood functions and normalizing by integration over the parameter variables, the form of the prior distribution has a significant influence on the posterior. This section gives some more details about the different types of prior distributions and guidelines as to which ones to use in a given context.

There are different ways of classifying prior distributions in a formal way. One of the approaches is based on how much information a prior provides. In this scheme, the prior distributions are classified as *Informative, Weakly Informative, Least Informative,* and *Non-informative*. A detailed discussion of each of these classes is beyond the scope of this book, and interested readers should consult relevant books (references 1 and 2 in the *References* section of this chapter). Here, we take more of a practitioner's approach and illustrate some of the important classes of the prior distributions commonly used in practice.

Non-informative priors

Let's start with the case where we do not have any prior knowledge about the model parameters. In this case, we want to express complete ignorance about model parameters through a mathematical expression. This is achieved through what are called non-informative priors. For example, in the case of a single random variable x that can take any value between $-\infty$ and $+\infty$, the non-informative prior for its mean μ would be the following:

$$P(\mu \mid m) \propto constant \ \forall - \infty < \mu < +\infty$$

Here, the complete ignorance of the parameter value is captured through a uniform distribution function in the parameter space. Note that a uniform distribution is not a proper distribution function since its integral over the domain is not equal to 1; therefore, it is not normalizable. However, one can use an improper distribution function for the prior as long as it is multiplied by the likelihood function; the resulting posterior can be normalized.

If the parameter of interest is variance σ^2, then by definition it can only take non-negative values. In this case, we transform the variable so that the transformed variable has a uniform probability in the range from $-\infty$ to $+\infty$:

$$x = \ln \sigma^2$$

$$P(x \mid m) \propto constant \ \forall -\infty < x < +\infty$$

It is easy to show, using simple differential calculus, that the corresponding non-informative distribution function in the original variable σ^2 would be as follows:

$$P(\sigma^2 \mid m) \propto \frac{1}{\sigma^2} \quad \forall \quad 0 < \sigma^2 < \infty$$

Another well-known non-informative prior used in practical applications is the Jeffreys prior, which is named after the British statistician Harold Jeffreys. This prior is invariant under reparametrization of θ and is defined as proportional to the square root of the determinant of the Fisher information matrix:

$$P(\theta) \propto \sqrt{\det I(\theta)}$$

Here, it is worth discussing the Fisher information matrix a little bit. If X is a random variable distributed according to $P(X \mid \theta)$, we may like to know how much information observations of X carry about the unknown parameter θ. This is what the Fisher Information Matrix provides. It is defined as the second moment of the score (first derivative of the logarithm of the likelihood function):

$$I(\theta) = E\left[\left(\frac{\partial}{\partial \theta} \log f(X; \theta) \right)^2 \mid \theta \right]$$

Let's take a simple two-dimensional problem to understand the Fisher information matrix and Jeffreys prior. This example is given by Prof. D. Wittman of the University of California (reference 3 in the *References* section of this chapter). Let's consider two types of food item: buns and hot dogs.

Let's assume that generally they are produced in pairs (a hot dog and bun pair), but occasionally hot dogs are also produced independently in a separate process. There are two observables such as the number of hot dogs (n_h) and the number of buns (n_b), and two model parameters such as the production rate of pairs (α) and the production rate of hot dogs alone (β). We assume that the uncertainty in the measurements of the counts of these two food products is distributed according to the normal distribution, with variance σ_h^2 and σ_b^2, respectively. In this case, the Fisher Information matrix for this problem would be as follows:

$$I(\sigma_h, \sigma_b) = \begin{bmatrix} \dfrac{1}{\sigma_h^2} + \dfrac{1}{\sigma_b^2} & \dfrac{1}{\sigma_h^2} \\ \dfrac{1}{\sigma_h^2} & \dfrac{1}{\sigma_h^2} \end{bmatrix}$$

In this case, the inverse of the Fisher information matrix would correspond to the covariance matrix:

$$\Sigma = \begin{bmatrix} \sigma_b^2 & -\sigma_b^2 \\ -\sigma_b^2 & \sigma_b^2 + \sigma_h^2 \end{bmatrix}$$

We have included one problem in the *Exercises* section of this chapter to compute the Fisher information matrix and Jeffrey's prior. Readers are requested to attempt this in order to get a feeling of how to compute Jeffrey's prior from observations.

Subjective priors

One of the key strengths of Bayesian statistics compared to classical (frequentist) statistics is that the framework allows one to capture subjective beliefs about any random variables. Usually, people will have intuitive feelings about minimum, maximum, mean, and most probable or peak values of a random variable. For example, if one is interested in the distribution of hourly temperatures in winter in a tropical country, then the people who are familiar with tropical climates or climatology experts will have a belief that, in winter, the temperature can go as low as 15°C and as high as 27°C with the most probable temperature value being 23°C. This can be captured as a prior distribution through the Triangle distribution as shown here.

The Triangle distribution has three parameters corresponding to a minimum value (a), the most probable value (b), and a maximum value (c). The mean and variance of this distribution are given by:

$$\mu = \frac{a+b+c}{3}$$

$$\sigma^2 = \frac{a^2 + b^2 + c^2 - ab - ac - bc}{18}$$

One can also use a PERT distribution to represent a subjective belief about the minimum, maximum, and most probable value of a random variable. The PERT distribution is a reparametrized Beta distribution, as follows:

$$PERT\left(x \mid a,b,c\right) = a + \left(c-a\right) * Beta\left(x \mid \alpha, \beta\right)$$

Here:

$$\alpha = \frac{\left(\mu - a\right)\left(2b - a - c\right)}{\left(b - \mu\right)\left(c - a\right)}$$

$$\beta = \frac{\alpha\left(c - \mu\right)}{\left(\mu - a\right)}$$

$$\mu = \frac{a + 4b + c}{6}$$

The PERT distribution is commonly used for project completion time analysis, and the name originates from project evaluation and review techniques. Another area where Triangle and PERT distributions are commonly used is in **risk modeling**.

Often, people also have a belief about the relative probabilities of values of a random variable. For example, when studying the distribution of ages in a population such as Japan or some European countries, where there are more old people than young, an expert could give relative weights for the probability of different ages in the populations. This can be captured through a relative distribution containing the following details:

$$\left[min, max, \{values\}, \{weights\} \right]$$

Here, *min* and *max* represent the minimum and maximum values, *{values}* represents the set of possible observed values, and *{weights}* represents their relative weights. For example, in the population age distribution problem, these could be the following:

$$\left[1, 114, \{5, 13, 18, 30, 45, 60, 75, 90\}, \{0.1, 0.3, 0.5, 0.3, 0.5, 0.6, 0.7, 0.4\} \right]$$

The weights need not have a sum of 1.

Conjugate priors

If both the prior and posterior distributions are in the same family of distributions, then they are called **conjugate distributions** and the corresponding prior is called a **conjugate prior for the likelihood function**. Conjugate priors are very helpful for getting get analytical closed-form expressions for the posterior distribution. In the simple example we considered, we saw that when the noise is distributed according to the normal distribution, choosing a normal prior for the mean resulted in a normal posterior. The following table gives examples of some well-known conjugate pairs that we will use in the later chapters of this book:

Likelihood function	Model parameters	Conjugate prior	Hyperparameters
Binomial	p (probability)	Beta	α, β
Poisson	λ (rate)	Gamma	k, θ

Categorical	p, k (probability, number of categories)	Dirichlet	α
Univariate normal (known variance σ^2)	μ (mean)	Normal	$\mu_0, \sigma_0^{\ 2}$
Univariate normal (known mean μ)	σ^2 (variance)	Inverse Gamma	α, β

Hierarchical priors

Sometimes, it is useful to define prior distributions for the hyperparameters itself. This is consistent with the Bayesian view that all parameters should be treated as uncertain by using probabilities. These distributions are called hyper-prior distributions. In theory, one can continue this into many levels as a hierarchical model. This is one way of eliciting the optimal prior distributions. For example:

$$P(\theta \mid X) = \frac{P(X \mid \theta) P(\theta \mid \alpha) P(\alpha)}{P(X)}$$

$P(\theta \mid \alpha)$ is the prior distribution with a hyperparameter α. We could define a prior distribution for α through a second set of equations, as follows:

$$P(\alpha) = P(\alpha \mid \beta) P(\beta)$$

Here, $P(\alpha \mid \beta)$ is the hyper-prior distribution for the hyperparameter α, parametrized by the hyper-hyper-parameter $\sigma_b^{\ 2}$. One can define a prior distribution for $\sigma_b^{\ 2}$ in the same way and continue the process forever. The practical reason for formalizing such models is that, at some level of hierarchy, one can define a uniform prior for the hyper parameters, reflecting complete ignorance about the parameter distribution, and effectively truncate the hierarchy. In practical situations, typically, this is done at the second level. This corresponds to, in the preceding example, using a uniform distribution for $P(\alpha \mid \beta)$.

I want to conclude this section by stressing one important point. Though prior distribution has a significant role in Bayesian inference, one need not worry about it too much, as long as the prior chosen is reasonable and consistent with the domain knowledge and evidence seen so far. The reasons are is that, first of all, as we have more evidence, the significance of the prior gets washed out. Secondly, when we use Bayesian models for prediction, we will average over the uncertainty in the estimation of the parameters using the posterior distribution. *This averaging is the key ingredient of Bayesian inference and it removes many of the ambiguities in the selection of the right prior.*

Estimation of posterior distribution

So far, we discussed the essential concept behind Bayesian inference and also how to choose a prior distribution. Since one needs to compute the posterior distribution of model parameters before one can use the models for prediction, we discuss this task in this section. Though the Bayesian rule has a very simple-looking form, the computation of posterior distribution in a practically usable way is often very challenging. This is primarily because computation of the normalization constant Z_N involves N-dimensional integrals, when there are N parameters. Even when one uses a conjugate prior, this computation can be very difficult to track analytically or numerically. This was one of the main reasons for not using Bayesian inference for multivariate modeling until recent decades. In this section, we will look at various approximate ways of computing posterior distributions that are used in practice.

Maximum a posteriori estimation

Maximum a posteriori (MAP) estimation is a point estimation that corresponds to taking the maximum value or mode of the posterior distribution. Though taking a point estimation does not capture the variability in the parameter estimation, it does take into account the effect of prior distribution to some extent when compared to maximum likelihood estimation. MAP estimation is also called poor man's Bayesian inference.

From the Bayes rule, we have:

$$\hat{\boldsymbol{\theta}}_{MAP} = \arg\max_{\theta} P(\boldsymbol{\theta} \mid X, m) = \arg\max_{\theta} P(X \mid \boldsymbol{\theta}, m) P(\boldsymbol{\theta} \mid m)$$

Here, for convenience, we have used the notation X for the N-dimensional vector $\{x_1, x_2, \cdots, x_N\}$. The last relation follows because the denominator of RHS of Bayes rule is independent of $\boldsymbol{\theta}$. Compare this with the following maximum likelihood estimate:

$$\hat{\boldsymbol{\theta}}_{ML} = \arg\max_{\theta} P(X \mid \boldsymbol{\theta}, m)$$

The difference between the MAP and ML estimate is that, whereas ML finds the mode of the likelihood function, MAP finds the mode of the product of the likelihood function and prior.

Laplace approximation

We saw that the MAP estimate just finds the maximum value of the posterior distribution. Laplace approximation goes one step further and also computes the local curvature around the maximum up to quadratic terms. This is equivalent to assuming that the posterior distribution is approximately Gaussian (normal) around the maximum. This would be the case if the amount of data were large compared to the number of parameters: $M >> N$.

$$P(\boldsymbol{\theta} \mid X, m) \approx (2\pi)^{-\frac{N}{2}} |A|^{\frac{1}{2}} \exp\left\{ -\frac{1}{2}(\boldsymbol{\theta} - \hat{\boldsymbol{\theta}})^T A(\boldsymbol{\theta} - \hat{\boldsymbol{\theta}}) \right\}$$

Here, A is an $N \times N$ Hessian matrix obtained by taking the derivative of the log of the posterior distribution:

$$A_{ij} = -\frac{\partial}{\partial \theta_i} \frac{\partial}{\partial \theta_j} \ln P(\boldsymbol{\theta} \mid X, m)_{|\theta = \hat{\theta}}$$

It is straightforward to evaluate the previous expressions at $\theta = \hat{\theta}$, using the following definition of conditional probability:

$$P(\boldsymbol{\theta} \mid X, m) = \frac{P(\boldsymbol{\theta}, X \mid m)}{P(X \mid m)}$$

We can get an expression for $P(X|m)$ from Laplace approximation that looks like the following:

$$\ln P(X|m) \approx \ln P(\hat{\theta}|m) + \ln P(X|\hat{\theta},m) + \frac{N}{2}\ln 2\pi - \frac{1}{2}\ln|A|$$

In the limit of a large number of samples, one can show that this expression simplifies to the following:

$$\ln P(X|m) \approx \ln P(X|\hat{\theta},m) - \frac{N}{2}\ln M$$

The term $-2\ln P(X|\hat{\theta},m) + N\ln M$ is called **Bayesian information criterion (BIC)** and can be used for model selections or model comparison. This is one of the **goodness of fit** terms for a statistical model. Another similar criterion that is commonly used is **Akaike information criterion (AIC)**, which is defined by $-2\ln P(X|\hat{\theta},m) + 2N$.

Now we will discuss how BIC can be used to compare different models for model selection. In the Bayesian framework, two models such as m_1 and m_2 are compared using the Bayes factor. The definition of the Bayes factor B_{12} is the ratio of posterior odds to prior odds that is given by:

$$B_{12} = \frac{P^{post}(m_1|X) / P^{post}(m_2|X)}{P^{prior}(m_1) / P^{prior}(m_2)}$$

Here, posterior odds is the ratio of posterior probabilities of the two models of the given data and prior odds is the ratio of prior probabilities of the two models, as given in the preceding equation. If $B_{12} > 1$, model m_1 is preferred by the data and if $B_{12} < 1$, model m_2 is preferred by the data.

In reality, it is difficult to compute the Bayes factor because it is difficult to get the precise prior probabilities. It can be shown that, in the large N limit, $(BIC(m_1) - BIC(m_2))$ can be viewed as a rough approximation to $-2\ln B_{12}$.

Monte Carlo simulations

The two approximations that we have discussed so far, the MAP and Laplace approximations, are useful when the posterior is a very sharply peaked function about the maximum value. Often, in real-life situations, the posterior will have long tails. This is, for example, the case in e-commerce where the probability of the purchasing of a product by a user has a long tail in the space of all products. So, in many practical situations, both MAP and Laplace approximations fail to give good results. Another approach is to directly sample from the posterior distribution. Monte Carlo simulation is a technique used for sampling from the posterior distribution and is one of the workhorses of Bayesian inference in practical applications. In this section, we will introduce the reader to **Markov Chain Monte Carlo (MCMC)** simulations and also discuss two common MCMC methods used in practice.

As discussed earlier, let $\theta = \{\theta_1, \theta_2, \cdots, \theta_N\}$ be the set of parameters that we are interested in estimating from the data through posterior distribution. Consider the case of the parameters being discrete, where each parameter has K possible values, that is, $\theta_i \in \{\theta_i^1, \theta_i^2, \cdots, \theta_i^K\}$. Set up a Markov process with states θ and transition probability matrix $T(\theta^{t+1} | \theta^t)$. The essential idea behind MCMC simulations is that one can choose the transition probabilities in such a way that the steady state distribution of the Markov chain would correspond to the posterior distribution we are interested in. Once this is done, sampling from the Markov chain output, after it has reached a steady state, will give samples of $\{\theta_1, \theta_2, \cdots, \theta_N\}$ distributed according to the posterior distribution.

Now, the question is how to set up the Markov process in such a way that its steady state distribution corresponds to the posterior of interest. There are two well-known methods for this. One is the Metropolis-Hastings algorithm and the second is Gibbs sampling. We will discuss both in some detail here.

The Metropolis-Hasting algorithm

The Metropolis-Hasting algorithm was one of the first major algorithms proposed for MCMC (reference 4 in the *References* section of this chapter). It has a very simple concept—something similar to a hill-climbing algorithm in optimization:

1.   Let θ^t be the state of the system at time step t.
2.   To move the system to another state at time step $t + 1$, generate a candidate state θ^* by sampling from a proposal distribution $q(\theta^* | \theta)$. The proposal distribution is chosen in such a way that it is easy to sample from it.

3. Accept the proposal move with the following probability:

$$\alpha = \min\left\{ 1, \frac{P(\theta^*)q(\theta \mid \theta^*)}{P(\theta)q(\theta^* \mid \theta)} \right\}$$

4. If it is accepted, $\theta^{t+1} = \theta^*$; if not, $\theta^{t+1} = \theta^t$.

5. Continue the process until the distribution converges to the steady state.

Here, $P(\theta)$ is the posterior distribution that we want to simulate. Under certain conditions, the preceding update rule will guarantee that, in the large time limit, the Markov process will approach a steady state distributed according to $P(\theta)$.

The intuition behind the Metropolis-Hasting algorithm is simple. The proposal distribution $q(\theta^* \mid \theta)$ gives the conditional probability of proposing state θ^* to make a transition in the next time step from the current state θ. Therefore, $q(\theta \mid \theta^*)P(\theta^*)$ is the probability that the system is currently in state θ^* and would make a transition to state θ in the next time step. Similarly, $q(\theta^* \mid \theta)P(\theta)$ is the probability that the system is currently in state θ and would make a transition to state θ^* in the next time step. If the ratio of these two probabilities is more than 1, accept the move. Alternatively, accept the move only with the probability given by the ratio. Therefore, the Metropolis-Hasting algorithm is like a hill-climbing algorithm where one accepts all the moves that are in the upward direction and accepts moves in the downward direction once in a while with a smaller probability. The downward moves help the system not to get stuck in local minima.

Let's revisit the example of estimating the posterior distribution of the mean and variance of the height of people in a population discussed in the introductory section. This time we will estimate the posterior distribution by using the Metropolis-Hasting algorithm. The following lines of R code do this job:

```
>set.seed(100)
>mu_t <- 5.5
>sd_t <- 0.5
>age_samples <- rnorm(10000,mean = mu_t,sd = sd_t)

>#function to compute log likelihood
>loglikelihood <- function(x,mu,sigma){
    singlell <- dnorm(x,mean = mu,sd = sigma,log = T)
    sumll <- sum(singlell)
    sumll
```

```
        }

>#function to compute prior distribution for mean on log scale
>d_prior_mu <- function(mu){
  dnorm(mu,0,10,log=T)
  }

>#function to compute prior distribution for std dev on log scale
>d_prior_sigma <- function(sigma){
  dunif(sigma,0,5,log=T)
  }

>#function to compute posterior distribution on log scale
>d_posterior <- function(x,mu,sigma){
  loglikelihood(x,mu,sigma) + d_prior_mu(mu) + d_prior_sigma(sigma)
    }

>#function to make transition moves
  tran_move <- function(x,dist = .1){
  x + rnorm(1,0,dist)
  }

>num_iter <- 10000
>posterior <- array(dim = c(2,num_iter))
>accepted <- array(dim=num_iter - 1)
>theta_posterior <-array(dim=c(2,num_iter))

>values_initial <- list(mu = runif(1,4,8),sigma = runif(1,1,5))
>theta_posterior[1,1] <- values_initial$mu
>theta_posterior[2,1] <- values_initial$sigma

>for (t in 2:num_iter){
   #proposed next values for parameters
    theta_proposed
              <- c(tran_move(theta_posterior[1,t-1])
              ,tran_move(theta_posterior[2,t-1]))
    p_proposed <- d_posterior(age_samples,mu = theta_proposed[1]
              ,sigma = theta_proposed[2])
    p_prev <-d_posterior(age_samples,mu = theta_posterior[1,t-1]
              ,sigma = theta_posterior[2,t-1])
    eps <- exp(p_proposed - p_prev)

    # proposal is accepted if posterior density is higher w/ theta_
proposed
```

```
        # if posterior density is not higher, it is accepted with
    probability eps
        accept <- rbinom(1,1,prob = min(eps,1))
        accepted[t - 1] <- accept
        if (accept == 1){
          theta_posterior[,t] <- theta_proposed
        } else {
          theta_posterior[,t] <- theta_posterior[,t-1]
        }
    }
}
```

To plot the resulting posterior distribution, we use the sm package in R:

```
>library(sm)
x <- cbind(c(theta_posterior[1,1:num_iter]),c(theta_posterior[2,1:num_
iter]))
xlim <- c(min(x[,1]),max(x[,1]))
ylim <- c(min(x[,2]),max(x[,2]))
zlim <- c(0,max(1))

sm.density(x,
           xlab = "mu",ylab="sigma",
           zlab = " ",zlim = zlim,
           xlim = xlim ,ylim = ylim,col="white")
title("Posterior density")
```

The resulting posterior distribution will look like the following figure:

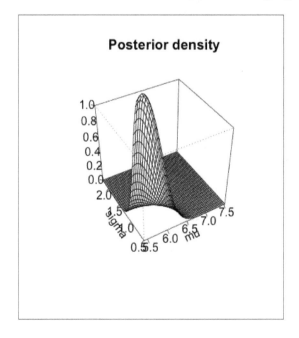

Though the Metropolis-Hasting algorithm is simple to implement for any Bayesian inference problem, in practice it may not be very efficient in many cases. The main reason for this is that, unless one carefully chooses a proposal distribution $q(\theta^*|\theta)$, there would be too many rejections and it would take a large number of updates to reach the steady state. This is particularly the case when the number of parameters are high. There are various modifications of the basic Metropolis-Hasting algorithms that try to overcome these difficulties. We will briefly describe these when we discuss various R packages for the Metropolis-Hasting algorithm in the following section.

R packages for the Metropolis-Hasting algorithm

There are several contributed packages in R for MCMC simulation using the Metropolis-Hasting algorithm, and here we describe some popular ones.

The **mcmc** package contributed by Charles J. Geyer and Leif T. Johnson is one of the popular packages in R for MCMC simulations. It has the `metrop` function for running the basic Metropolis-Hasting algorithm. The `metrop` function uses a multivariate normal distribution as the proposal distribution.

Sometimes, it is useful to make a variable transformation to improve the speed of convergence in MCMC. The mcmc package has a function named `morph` for doing this. Combining these two, the function `morph.metrop` first transforms the variable, does a Metropolis on the transformed density, and converts the results back to the original variable.

Apart from the mcmc package, two other useful packages in R are **MHadaptive** contributed by Corey Chivers and the **Evolutionary Monte Carlo (EMC) algorithm** package by Gopi Goswami. Due to lack of space, we will not be discussing these two packages in this book. Interested readers are requested to download these from the C-RAN project's site and experiment with them.

Gibbs sampling

As mentioned before, the Metropolis-Hasting algorithm suffers from the drawback of poor convergence, due to too many rejections, if one does not choose a good proposal distribution. To avoid this problem, two physicists Stuart Geman and Donald Geman proposed a new algorithm (reference 5 in the *References* section of this chapter). This algorithm is called Gibbs sampling and it is named after the famous physicist J W Gibbs. Currently, Gibbs sampling is the workhorse of MCMC for Bayesian inference.

Let $\theta = \{\theta_1, \theta_2, \cdots, \theta_N\}$ be the set of parameters of the model that we wish to estimate:

1. Start with an initial state $\theta^0 = \{\theta_1^0, \theta_2^0, \cdots, \theta_N^0\}$.

2. At each time step, update the components one by one, by drawing from a distribution conditional on the most recent value of rest of the components:

$$\theta_1^{t+1} \sim P\left(\theta_1 \mid \theta_2^t, \cdots, \theta_N^t\right)$$

$$\theta_2^{t+1} \sim P\left(\theta_2 \mid \theta_1^{t+1}, \theta_3^t \cdots, \theta_N^t\right)$$

$$\cdots$$

$$\theta_2^{t+1} \sim P\left(\theta_i \mid \theta_1^{t+1}, \cdots \theta_{i-1}^{t+1}, \theta_{i+1}^t \cdots, \theta_N^t\right)$$

$$\cdots$$

$$\theta_N^{t+1} \sim P\left(\theta_N \mid \theta_1^{t+1}, \cdots, \theta_{N-1}^{t+1}\right)$$

3. After N steps, all components of the parameter will be updated.

4. Continue with step 2 until the Markov process converges to a steady state.

Gibbs sampling is a very efficient algorithm since there are no rejections. However, to be able to use Gibbs sampling, the form of the conditional distributions of the posterior distribution should be known.

R packages for Gibbs sampling

Unfortunately, there are not many contributed general purpose Gibbs sampling packages in R. The **gibbs.met** package provides two generic functions for performing MCMC in a Naïve way for user-defined target distribution. The first function is `gibbs_met`. This performs Gibbs sampling with each 1-dimensional distribution sampled by using the Metropolis algorithm, with normal distribution as the proposal distribution. The second function, `met_gaussian`, updates the whole state with independent normal distribution centered around the previous state. The gibbs.met package is useful for general purpose MCMC on moderate dimensional problems.

In the *Exercises* section of this chapter, we will discuss one problem that involves sampling from the two-dimensional normal distribution by using both the Metropolis-Hasting algorithm and Gibbs sampling to make these concepts more clear. Readers can use these mentioned packages for solving this exercise.

Apart from the general purpose MCMC packages, there are several packages in R designed to solve a particular type of machine-learning problems. The **GibbsACOV** package can be used for one-way mixed-effects ANOVA and ANCOVA models. The **lda** package performs collapsed Gibbs sampling methods for topic (LDA) models. The **stocc** package fits a spatial occupancy model via Gibbs sampling. The **binomlogit** package implements an efficient MCMC for Binomial Logit models. **Bmk** is a package for doing diagnostics of MCMC output. **Bayesian Output Analysis Program (BOA)** is another similar package. **RBugs** is an interface of the well-known **OpenBUGS** MCMC package. The **ggmcmc** package is a graphical tool for analyzing MCMC simulation. **MCMCglm** is a package for generalized linear mixed models and **BoomSpikeSlab** is a package for doing MCMC for Spike and Slab regression. Finally, **SamplerCompare** is a package (more of a framework) for comparing the performance of various MCMC packages.

Variational approximation

In the variational approximation scheme, one assumes that the posterior distribution $P(\theta_1, \theta_2, \cdots, \theta_N \mid X)$ can be approximated to a factorized form:

$$P\left(\theta_1, \theta_2, \cdots, \theta_N \mid X\right) \approx Q\left(\theta_1, \theta_2, \cdots, \theta_N \mid X\right) = \prod_{i=1}^{N} q_i\left(\theta_i \mid X\right)$$

Note that the factorized form is also a conditional distribution, so each θ_i can have dependence on other θ_js through the conditioned variable X. In other words, this is not a trivial factorization making each parameter independent. The advantage of this factorization is that one can choose more analytically tractable forms of distribution functions $q_i(\theta_i \mid X)$. In fact, one can vary the functions $\{q_i(\theta_i \mid X)\}$ in such a way that it is as close to the true posterior $P(\theta_1, \theta_2, \cdots, \theta_N \mid X)$ as possible. This is mathematically formulated as a **variational calculus** problem, as explained here.

Let's use some measures to compute the distance between the two probability distributions, such as $P(\boldsymbol{\theta} \mid X)$ and $Q(\boldsymbol{\theta} \mid X)$, where $\theta = \{\theta_1, \theta_2, \cdots, \theta_N\}$. One of the standard measures of distance between probability distributions is the Kullback-Leibler divergence, or KL-divergence for short. It is defined as follows:

$$D_{KL}\left(Q \| P\right) = \sum_{\theta} Q\left(\boldsymbol{\theta} \mid X\right) \ln\left[\frac{Q\left(\boldsymbol{\theta} \mid X\right)}{P\left(\boldsymbol{\theta} \mid X\right)}\right]$$

The reason why it is called a divergence and not distance is that $D_{KL}(Q\|P)$ is not symmetric with respect to Q and P. One can use the relation $P(X,\theta)=P(\theta|X)P(X)$ and rewrite the preceding expression as an equation for *log P(X)*:

$$\ln P(X) = D_{KL}(Q\|P) + \mathcal{L}(Q)$$

Here:

$$\mathcal{L}(Q) = -\sum_{\theta} Q(\theta|X)\ln\left[\frac{Q(\theta|X)}{P(X,\theta)}\right]$$

Note that, in the equation for *ln P(X)*, there is no dependence on Q on the LHS. Therefore, maximizing $\mathcal{L}(Q)$ with respect to Q will minimize $D_{KL}(Q\|P)$, since their sum is a term independent of Q. By choosing analytically tractable functions for Q, one can do this maximization in practice. It will result in both an approximation for the posterior and a lower bound for *ln P(X)* that is the logarithm of evidence or marginal likelihood, since $P(X)=\int P(X|\theta)P(\theta)d\theta$.

Therefore, variational approximation gives us two quantities in one shot. A posterior distribution can be used to make predictions about future observations (as explained in the next section) and a lower bound for evidence can be used for model selection.

How does one implement this minimization of KL-divergence in practice? Without going into mathematical details, here we write a final expression for the solution:

$$q_j*(\theta_j|X) = \frac{\exp\left\{E_{i\neq j}\left[\ln P(X,\theta)\right]\right\}}{\int \exp\left\{E_{i\neq j}\left[\ln P(X,\theta)\right]\right\}d\theta_j}$$

Here, $E_{i\neq j}\left[\ln P(X,\theta)\right]$ implies that the expectation of the logarithm of the joint distribution $P(X,\theta)$ is taken over all the parameters $\{\theta_i\}$ except for θ_j. Therefore, the minimization of KL-divergence leads to a set of coupled equations; one for each $q_i*(\theta_i|X)$ needs to be solved self-consistently to obtain the final solution. Though the variational approximation looks very complex mathematically, it has a very simple, intuitive explanation. The posterior distribution of each parameter θ_i is obtained by averaging the log of the joint distribution over all the other variables. This is analogous to the Mean Field theory in physics where, if there are N interacting charged particles, the system can be approximated by saying that each particle is in a constant external field, which is the average of fields produced by all the other particles.

We will end this section by mentioning a few R packages for variational approximation. The **VBmix** package can be used for variational approximation in Bayesian mixture models. A similar package is **vbdm** used for Bayesian discrete mixture models. The package **vbsr** is used for variational inference in Spike Regression Regularized Linear Models.

Prediction of future observations

Once we have the posterior distribution inferred from data using some of the methods described already, it can be used to predict future observations. The probability of observing a value Y, given observed data X, and posterior distribution of parameters $P(\theta|X,m)$ is given by:

$$P(Y|X,m) = \int P(Y|X,\theta,m)P(\theta|X,m)\,d\theta$$

Note that, in this expression, the likelihood function $P(Y|X,\theta,m)$ is averaged by using the distribution of the parameter given by the posterior $P(\theta|X,m)$. This is, in fact, the core strength of the Bayesian inference. This Bayesian averaging eliminates the uncertainty in estimating the parameter values and makes the prediction more robust.

Exercises

1. Derive the equation for the posterior mean by expanding the square in the exponential $(h_i - \mu)^2$ for each i, collecting all similar power terms, and making a perfect square again. Note that the product of exponentials can be written as the exponential of a sum of terms.

2. For this exercise, we use the dataset corresponding to Smartphone-Based Recognition of Human Activities and Postural Transitions, from the UCI Machine Learning repository (https://archive.ics.uci.edu/ml/datasets/Smartphone-Based+Recognition+of+Human+Activities+and+Postural+Transitions). It contains values of acceleration taken from an accelerometer on a smartphone. The original dataset contains x, y, and z components of the acceleration and the corresponding timestamp values. For this exercise, we have used only the two horizontal components of the acceleration x and y. In this exercise, let's assume that the acceleration follows a normal distribution. Let's also assume a normal prior distribution for the mean values of acceleration with a hyperparameter for a mean that is uniformly distributed in the interval (-0.5, 0.5) and a known variance equal to 1. Find the posterior mean value by using the expression given in the equation.

3. Write an R function to compute the Fisher information matrix. Obtain the Fisher information matrix for this problem by using the dataset mentioned in exercise 1 of this section.

4. Set up an MCMC simulation for this problem by using the **mcmc** package in R. Plot a histogram of the simulated data.

5. Set up an MCMC simulation using Gibbs sampling. Compare the results with that of the Metropolis algorithm.

References

1. Berger J.O. *Statistical Decision Theory and Bayesian Analysis*. Springer Series in Statistics. 1993. ISBN-10: 0387960988

2. Jayes E.T. *Probability Theory: The Logic of Science*. Cambridge University Press. 2003. ISBN-10: 052159271

3. Wittman D. "Fisher Matrix for Beginners". Physics Department, University of California at Davis (http://www.physics.ucdavis.edu/~dwittman/Fisher-matrix-guide.pdf)

4. Metropolis N, Rosenbluth A.W., Rosenbluth M.N., Teller A.H., Teller E. "Equations of State Calculations by Fast Computing Machines". Journal of Chemical Physics 21 (6): 1087–1092. 1953

5. Geman S., Geman D. "Stochastic Relaxation, Gibbs Distributions, and the Bayesian Restoration of Images". IEEE Transactions on Pattern Analysis and Machine Intelligence 6 (6): 721-741. 1984

Summary

In this chapter, we covered basic principles of Bayesian inference. Starting with how uncertainty is treated differently in Bayesian statistics compared to classical statistics, we discussed deeply various components of Bayes' rule. Firstly, we learned the different types of prior distributions and how to choose the right one for your problem. Then we learned the estimation of posterior distribution using techniques such as MAP estimation, Laplace approximation, and MCMC simulations. Once the readers have comprehended this chapter, they will be in a position to apply Bayesian principles in their data analytics problems. Before we start discussing specific Bayesian machine learning problems, in the next chapter, we will review machine learning in general.

4
Machine Learning Using Bayesian Inference

Now that we have learned about Bayesian inference and R, it is time to use both for machine learning. In this chapter, we will give an overview of different machine learning techniques and discuss each of them in detail in subsequent chapters. Machine learning is a field at the intersection of computer science and statistics, and a subbranch of artificial intelligence or AI. The name essentially comes from the early works in AI where researchers were trying to develop learning machines that automatically learned the relationship between input and output variables from data alone. Once a machine is trained on a dataset for a given problem, it can be used as a black box to predict values of output variables for new values of input variables.

It is useful to set this learning process of a machine in a mathematical framework. Let X and Y be two random variables such that we seek a learning machine that learns the relationship between these two variables from data and predicts the value of Y, given the value of X. The system is fully characterized by a joint probability distribution $P(X, Y)$, however, the form of this distribution is unknown. The goal of learning is to find a function $f(X)$, which maps from X to Y, such that the predictions $\hat{Y} = f(X)$ contain as small error as possible. To achieve this, one chooses a loss function $L(Y, f(X))$ and finds an $f(X)$ that minimizes the expected or average loss over the joint distribution of X and Y given by:

$$E[L] = \int L(Y, f(X)) P(X, Y) dX \ dY$$

In Statistical Decision Theory, this is called **empirical risk minimization**. The typical loss function used is **square loss function** ($L(Y, f(X)) = (Y - f(X))^2$), if Y is a continuous variable, and **Hinge loss function** ($L(Y, f(X)) = max(0, 1 - Yf(X))$), if Y is a binary discrete variable with values ± 1. The first case is typically called **regression** and second case is called **binary classification**, as we will see later in this chapter.

The mathematical framework described here is called **supervised learning**, where the machine is presented with a training dataset containing ground truth values corresponding to pairs (Y, X). Let us consider the case of square loss function again. Here, the learning task is to find an $f(X)$ that minimizes the following:

$$E[L] = \int (Y - f(X))^2 P(Y \mid X) P(X) dX \ dY$$

Since the objective is to predict values of Y for the given values of X, we have used the conditional distribution $P(Y \mid X)$ inside the integral using factorization of $P(X, Y)$. It can be shown that the minimization of the preceding loss function leads to the following solution:

$$\hat{f}(X) = \mathbf{E}\left[(Y \mid X)\right] = \int Y P(Y \mid X) dY$$

The meaning of the preceding equation is that the best prediction of Y for any input value X is the mean or expectation denoted by E, of the conditional probability distribution $P(Y \mid X)$ conditioned at X.

In *Chapter 3, Introducing Bayesian Inference*, we mentioned **maximum likelihood estimation** (**MLE**) as a method for learning the parameters Θ of any distribution $P(X)$. In general, MLE is the same as the minimization of a square loss function if the underlying distribution is a normal distribution.

Note that, in empirical risk minimization, we are learning the parameter, $E[(Y \mid X)]$, the mean of the conditional distribution, for a given value of X. We will use one particular machine learning task, linear regression, to explain the advantage of Bayesian inference over the classical method of learning. However, before this, we will briefly explain some more general aspects of machine learning.

There are two types of supervised machine learning models, namely generative models and discriminative models. In the case of generative models, the algorithm tries to learn the joint probability of X and Y, which is $P(X,Y)$, from data and uses it to estimate mean $P(Y|X)$. In the case of discriminative models, the algorithm tries to directly learn the desired function, which is the mean of $P(Y|X)$, and no modeling of the X variable is attempted.

Labeling values of the target variable in the training data is done manually. This makes supervised learning very expensive when one needs to use very large datasets as in the case of text analytics. However, very often, supervised learning methods produce the most accurate results.

If there is not enough training data available for learning, one can still use machine learning through **unsupervised learning**. Here, the learning is mainly through the discovery of patterns of associations between variables in the dataset. Clustering data points that have similar features is a classic example.

Reinforcement learning is the third type of machine learning, where the learning takes place in a dynamic environment where the machine needs to perform certain actions based on its current state. Associated with each action is a reward. The machine needs to learn what action needs to be taken at each state so that the total reward is maximized. This is typically how a robot learns to perform tasks, such as driving a vehicle, in a real-life environment.

Why Bayesian inference for machine learning?

We have already discussed the advantages of Bayesian statistics over classical statistics in the last chapter. In this chapter, we will see in more detail how some of the concepts of Bayesian inference that we learned in the last chapter are useful in the context of machine learning. For this purpose, we take one simple machine learning task, namely linear regression. Let us consider a learning task where we have a dataset D containing N pair of points (X_i, Y_i) and the goal is to build a machine learning model using linear regression that it can be used to predict values of Y_i, given new values of X_i.

In linear regression, first, we assume that Y is of the following form:

$$Y_i = F(X_i) + \epsilon_i$$

Here, $F(X)$ is a function that captures the true relationship between X and Y, and ϵ is an error term that captures the inherent noise in the data. It is assumed that this noise is characterized by a normal distribution with mean 0 and variance σ_ϵ^2. What this implies is that if we have an infinite training dataset, we can learn the form of $F(X)$ from data and, even then, we can only predict Y up to an additive noise term ϵ. In practice, we will have only a finite training dataset D; hence, we will be able to learn only an approximation for $F(X)$ denoted by $f_D(X)$.

Note that we are discussing two types of errors here. One is an error term ϵ that is due to the inherent noise in the data that we cannot do much about. The second error is in learning $F(X)$, approximately through the function $f_D(X)$ from the dataset D.

In general, $f_D(X)$, which the approximate mapping between input variable X and output variable Y, is a function of X with a set of parameters Θ. When $f_D(X)$ is a linear function of the parameters Θ, we say the learning model is linear. It is a general misconception that linear regression corresponds to the case only if $f_D(X)$ is a linear function of X. The reason for linearity in the parameter and not in X is that, during the minimization of the loss function, one actually minimizes over the parameter values to find the best $f_D(X)$. Hence, a function that is linear in Θ will lead to a linear optimization problem that can be tackled analytically and numerically more easily. Therefore, linear regression corresponds to the following:

$$f_D(X) = \theta_1 b_1(X) + \theta_2 b_2(X) + \cdots + \theta_M b_M(X)$$

This is an expansion over a set of M basis functions $\{b_i(X)\}$. Here, each basis function $b_i(X)$ is a function of X without any unknown parameters. In machine learning, these are called feature functions or model features. For the linear regression problem, the loss function, therefore, can be written as follows:

$$E[L] = \frac{1}{2} \sum_{i=1}^{N} \left(Y_i - f_D(X_i)\right)^2 = \frac{1}{2} \sum_{i=1}^{N} \left(Y_i - \Theta^T B(X_i)\right)^2$$

Here, Θ^T is the transpose of the parameter vector $\Theta = \{\theta_1, \theta_2, \cdots, \theta_M\}$ and $B(X)$ is the vector composed of the basis functions $B(X) = \{b_1(X), b_2(X), \cdots, b_M(X)\}$. Learning $f_D(X)$ from a dataset implies estimating the values of Θ by minimizing the loss function through some optimization schemes such as gradient descent.

It is important to choose as many basis functions as possible to capture interesting patterns in the data. However, choosing more numbers of basis functions or features will overfit the model in the sense that it will even start fitting the noise contained in the data. Overfit will lead to poor predictions on new input data. Therefore, it is important to choose an optimum number of best features to maximize the predictive accuracy of any machine learning model. In machine learning based on classical statistics, this is achieved through what is called **bias-variance tradeoff** and **model regularization**. Whereas, in machine learning through Bayesian inference, accuracy of a predictive model can be maximized through Bayesian model averaging, and there is no need to impose model regularization or bias-variance tradeoff. We will learn each of these concepts in the following sections.

Model overfitting and bias-variance tradeoff

The expected loss mentioned in the previous section can be written as a sum of three terms in the case of linear regression using squared loss function, as follows:

$$Expected\ Loss = Bias^2 + Variance + Noise$$

Here, *Bias* is the difference $(F(X) - E_D[f_D(X)])$ between the true model *F(X)* and average value of $f_D(X)$ taken over an ensemble of datasets. *Bias* is a measure of how much the average prediction over all datasets in the ensemble differs from the true regression function *F(X)*. *Variance* is given by $E_D\left[(f_D(X) - E_D[f_D(X)])^2\right]$. It is a measure of extent to which the solution for a given dataset varies around the mean over all datasets. Hence, *Variance* is a measure of how much the function $f_D(X)$ is sensitive to the particular choice of dataset *D*. The third term *Noise*, as mentioned earlier, is the expectation of difference $(Y - F(X))$ between observation and the true regression function, over all the values of *X* and *Y*. Putting all these together, we can write the following:

$$E[L] = \left(F(X) - E_D[f_D(X)]\right)^2 + E_D\left[\left(f_D(X) - E_D[f_D(X)]\right)^2\right] + E_{XY}\left(Y - F(X)\right)$$

The objective of machine learning is to learn the function $f_D(X)$ from data that minimizes the expected loss $E[L]$. One can keep minimizing the bias by keeping more and more basis functions in the model and thereby increasing the model's complexity. However, since each of the model parameters $\{\theta\}$ are learned from a given dataset, the more complex the model becomes, the more sensitive its parameter estimation would be to the dataset used. This results in increased variance for more complex models. Hence, in any supervised machine learning task, there is a tradeoff between model bias and model complexity. One has to choose a model of optimum complexity to minimize the error of prediction on an unseen dataset. In the classical or frequentist approach, this is done by partitioning the labeled data into three sets. One is the training set, the second is the validation set, and the third is the test set. Models of different complexity that are trained using the training set are evaluated using the validation dataset to choose the model with optimum complexity. It is then, finally, evaluated against the test set to estimate the prediction error.

Selecting models of optimum complexity

There are different ways of selecting models with the right complexity so that the prediction error on unseen data is less. Let's discuss each of these approaches in the context of the linear regression model.

Subset selection

In the subset selection approach, one selects only a subset of the whole set of variables, which are significant, for the model. This not only increases the prediction accuracy of the model by decreasing model variance, but it is also useful from the interpretation point of view. There are different ways of doing subset selection, but the following two are the most commonly used approaches:

- **Forward selection**: In forward selection, one starts with no variables (intercept alone), and by using a greedy algorithm, adds other variables one by one. For each step, the variable that most improves the fit is chosen to add to the model.

- **Backward selection**: In backward selection, one starts with the full model and sequentially deletes the variable that has the least impact on the fit. At each step, the variable with the least Z-score is selected for elimination. In statistics, the Z-score of a random variable is a measure of the standard deviation between an element and its mean. A small value of Z-score (typically < 2) indicates that the effect of the variable is more likely by chance and is not statistically significant.

Model regularization

In this approach, one adds a penalty term to the loss function that does not allow the size of the parameter to become very large during minimization. There are two main ways of doing this:

- **Ridge regression**: This simple type of regularization is where the additional term is proportional to the magnitude of the parameter vector given by $\Theta^T \Theta$. The loss function for linear regression with the regularization term can be written as follows:

$$\frac{1}{2}\sum_{i=1}^{N}\left(Yi-\Theta^T B\left(X_i\right)\right)^2 + \frac{\lambda}{2}\Theta^T \Theta$$

  Parameters θ_i having a large magnitude will contribute more to the loss. Hence, minimization of the preceding loss function will typically produce parameters having small values and reduce the overfit. The optimum value of λ is found from the validation set.

- **Lasso**: In Lasso also, one adds a penalty term similar to ridge regression, but the term is proportional to the sum of modulus of each parameter and not its square:

$$\frac{1}{2}\sum_{i=1}^{N}\left(Y_i-\Theta^T B\left(X_i\right)\right)^2 + \frac{\lambda}{2}\sum_{i=1}^{N}\left|\Theta_i\right|$$

Though this looks like a simple change, Lasso has some very important differences with respect to ridge regression. First of all, the presence of the $\left|\Theta_i\right|$ term makes the loss function nonlinear in parameters Θ. The corresponding minimization problem is called the quadratic programming problem compared to the linear programming problem in ridge regression, for which a closed form solution is available. Due to the particular form $\left|\Theta_i\right|$ of the penalty, when the coefficients shrink as a result of minimization, some of them eventually become zero. So, Lasso is also in some sense a subset selection problem.

A detailed discussion of various subset selection and model regularization approaches can be found in the book by Trevor Hastie et.al (reference 1 in the *References* section of this chapter).

Bayesian averaging

So far, we have learned that simply minimizing the loss function (or equivalently maximizing the log likelihood function in the case of normal distribution) is not enough to develop a machine learning model for a given problem. One has to worry about models overfitting the training data, which will result in larger prediction errors on new datasets. The main advantage of Bayesian methods is that one can, in principle, get away from this problem, without using explicit regularization and different datasets for training and validation. This is called Bayesian model averaging and will be discussed here. This is one of the answers to our main question of the chapter, *why Bayesian inference for machine learning?*

For this, let's do a full Bayesian treatment of the linear regression problem. Since we only want to explain how Bayesian inference avoids the overfitting problem, we will skip all the mathematical derivations and state only the important results here. For more details, interested readers can refer to the book by Christopher M. Bishop (reference 2 in the *References* section of this chapter).

The linear regression equation $Y = f(X) + \epsilon$, with ϵ having a normal distribution with zero mean and variance σ^2 (equivalently, precision $\beta = 1/\sigma^2$), can be cast in a probability distribution form with Y having a normal distribution with mean $f(X)$ and precision β. Therefore, linear regression is equivalent to estimating the mean of the normal distribution:

$$P(Y \mid X) = N\left(Y \mid f(X), \beta^{-1}\right)$$

Since $f(X) = \Theta^T B(X)$, where the set of basis functions $B(X)$ is known and we are assuming here that the noise parameter β is also a known constant, only Θ needs to be taken as an uncertain variable for a fully Bayesian treatment.

The first step in Bayesian inference is to compute a posterior distribution of parameter vector Θ. For this, we assume that the prior distribution of Θ is an M dimensional normal distribution (since there are M components) with mean μ_0 and covariance matrix Σ_0. As we have seen in *Chapter 3, Introducing Bayesian Inference,* this corresponds to taking a conjugate distribution for the prior:

$$P(\Theta) = N\left(\Theta \mid \mu_0, \Sigma_0\right)$$

The corresponding posterior distribution is given by:

$$P(\Theta \mid Y) = N(\Theta \mid \boldsymbol{\mu_N}, \boldsymbol{\Sigma_N})$$

Here, $\mu_N = \Sigma_N \left(\Sigma_0^{-1} \mu_0 + \beta B^T Y \right)$ and $\Sigma_N^{-1} = \Sigma_0^{-1} + \beta B^T B$.

Here, B is an N x M matrix formed by stacking basis vectors B, at different values of X, on top of each other as shown here:

$$\begin{bmatrix} b_1(X_1) & \cdots & b_M(X_1) \\ \vdots & \ddots & \vdots \\ b_1(X_N) & \cdots & b_M(X_N) \end{bmatrix}$$

Now that we have the posterior distribution for Θ as a closed-form analytical expression, we can use it to predict new values of Y. To get an analytical closed-form expression for the predictive distribution of Y, we make an assumption that $\mu_0 = 0$ and $\Sigma_0 = \alpha^{-1} \boldsymbol{I}$. This corresponds to a prior with zero mean and isotropic covariance matrix characterized by one precision parameter α. The predictive distribution or the probability that the prediction for a new value of $X = x$ is y, is given by:

$$P(y \mid x) = \int P(y \mid \Theta^T B(x)) P(\Theta \mid Y, \alpha, \beta) d\Theta$$

This equation is the central theme of this section. In the classical or frequentist approach, one estimates a particular value $\hat{\Theta}$ for the parameter Θ from the training dataset and finds the probability of predicting y by simply using $P(y \mid \hat{\Theta}^T B(x))$. This does not address the overfitting of the model unless regularization is used. In Bayesian inference, we are integrating out the parameter variable Θ by using its posterior probability distribution $P(\Theta \mid Y, \alpha, \beta)$ learned from the data. This averaging will remove the necessity of using regularization or keeping the parameters to an optimal level through bias-variance tradeoff. This can be seen from the closed-form expression for $P(y \mid x)$, after we substitute the expressions for $P(y \mid \Theta^T B(x))$ and $P(\Theta \mid Y, \alpha, \beta)$ for the linear regression problem and do the integration. Since both are normal distributions, the integration can be done analytically that results in the following simple expression for $P(y \mid x)$:

$$P(y \mid x) = N\left(y \mid \boldsymbol{\mu_N}^T B(x), \sigma_N^2(x)\right)$$

Here, $\sigma_N^2(x) = \dfrac{1}{\beta} + B(x)^T \Sigma_N B(x)$.

This equation implies that the variance of the predictive distribution consists of two terms. One term, $1/\beta$, coming from the inherent noise in the data and the second term coming from the uncertainty associated with the estimation of model parameter Θ from data. One can show that as the size of training data N becomes very large, the second term decreases and in the limit $N \to \infty$ it becomes zero.

The example shown here illustrates the power of Bayesian inference. Since one can take care of uncertainty in the parameter estimation through Bayesian averaging, one doesn't need to keep separate validation data and all the data can be used for training. So, a full Bayesian treatment of a problem avoids the overfitting issue. Another major advantage of Bayesian inference, which we will not go into in this section, is treating latent variables in a machine learning model. In the next section, we will give a high-level overview of the various common machine learning tasks.

An overview of common machine learning tasks

This section is a prequel to the following chapters, where we will discuss different machine learning techniques in detail. At a high level, there are only a handful of tasks that machine learning tries to address. However, for each of such tasks, there are several approaches and algorithms in place.

The typical tasks in any machine learning are one of the following:

- Classification
- Regression
- Clustering
- Association rules
- Forecasting
- Dimensional reduction
- Density estimation

In classification, the objective is to assign a new data point to one of the predetermined classes. Typically, this is either a supervised or semi-supervised learning problem. The well-known machine learning algorithms used for classification are logistic regression, **support vector machines** (**SVM**), decision trees, Naïve Bayes, neural networks, Adaboost, and random forests. Here, Naïve Bayes is a Bayesian inference-based method. Other algorithms, such as logistic regression and neural networks, have also been implemented in the Bayesian framework.

Regression is probably the most common machine learning problem. It is used to determine the relation between a set of input variables (typically, continuous variables) and an output (dependent) variable that is continuous. We discussed the simplest example of linear regression in some detail in the previous section. More complex examples of regression are generalized linear regression, spline regression, nonlinear regression using neural networks, support vector regression, and Bayesian network. Bayesian formulations of regression include the Bayesian network and Bayesian linear regression.

Clustering is a classic example of unsupervised learning. Here, the objective is to group together similar items in a dataset based on certain features of the data. The number of clusters is not known in advance. Hence, clustering is more of a pattern detection problem. The well-known clustering algorithms are K-means clustering, hierarchical clustering, and **Latent Dirichlet allocation** (**LDA**). In this, LDA is formulated as a Bayesian inference problem. Other clustering methods using Bayesian inference include the Bayesian mixture model.

Association rule mining is an unsupervised method that finds items that are co-occurring in large transactions of data. The market basket analysis, which finds the items that are sold together in a supermarket, is based on association rule mining. The Apriori algorithm and frequent pattern matching algorithm are two main methods used for association rule mining.

Forecasting is similar to regression, except that the data is a time series where there are observations with different values of time stamp and the objective is to predict future values based on the current and past values. For this purpose, one can use methods such as ARIMA, neural networks, and dynamic Bayesian networks.

One of the fundamental issues in machine learning is called *the curse of dimensionality*. Since there can be a large number of features in a machine learning model, the typical minimization of error that one has to do to estimate model parameters will involve search and optimization in a large dimensional space. Most often, data will be very sparse in this higher dimensional space. This can make the search for optimal parameters very inefficient. To avoid this problem, one tries to project this higher dimensional space into a lower dimensional space containing a few important variables. One can then use these lower dimensional variables as features. The two well-known examples of dimensional reduction are principal component analysis and self-organized maps.

Often, the probability distribution of a population is directly estimated, without any parametric models, from a small amount of observed data for making inferences. This is called **density estimation**. The simplest form of density estimation is histograms, though it is not adequate for many practical applications. The more sophisticated density estimations are **kernel density estimation** (**KDE**) and vector quantization.

References

1. Friedman J., Hastie T., and Tibshirani R. *The Elements of Statistical Learning – Data Mining, Inference, and Prediction.* Springer Series in Statistics. 2009

2. Bishop C.M. *Pattern Recognition and Machine Learning (Information Science and Statistics).* Springer. 2006. ISBN-10: 0387310738

Summary

In this chapter, we got an overview of what machine learning is and what some of its high-level tasks are. We also discussed the importance of Bayesian inference in machine learning, particularly in the context of how it can help to avoid important issues, such as model overfit and how to select optimum models. In the coming chapters, we will learn some of the Bayesian machine learning methods in detail.

5
Bayesian Regression Models

In the previous chapter, we covered the theory of Bayesian linear regression in some detail. In this chapter, we will take a sample problem and illustrate how it can be applied to practical situations. For this purpose, we will use the **generalized linear model (GLM)** packages in R. Firstly, we will give a brief introduction to the concept of GLM to the readers.

Generalized linear regression

Recall that in linear regression, we assume the following functional form between the dependent variable Y and independent variable X:

$$Y = \Theta^T B(X) + \in$$

Here, $B(X) = \{b_1(X), b_2(X), \cdots, b_M(X)\}$ is a set of basis functions and $\Theta = \{\theta_1, \theta_2, \cdots, \theta_M\}$ is the parameter vector. Usually, it is assumed that $b_1(X) = 1$, so θ_1 represents an intercept or a bias term. Also, it is assumed that $\in$ is a noise term distributed according to the normal distribution with mean zero and variance σ^2. We also showed that this results in the following equation:

$$\mathbb{E}[Y \mid X] = \Theta^T B(X)$$

One can generalize the preceding equation to incorporate not only the normal distribution for noise but any distribution in the exponential family (reference 1 in the *References* section of this chapter). This is done by defining the following equation:

$$\mathbb{E}[Y \mid X] = \mu = g^{-1}\left(\Theta^{T} B(X)\right)$$

Here, g is called a link function. The well-known models, such as logistic regression, log-linear models, Poisson regression, and so on, are special cases of GLM. For example, in the case of ordinary linear regression, the link function would be $g(\mu) = \mu$. For logistic regression, it is $g(\mu) = logit(\mu)$, which is the inverse of the logistic function, and for Poisson regression, it is $g(\mu) = log(\mu)$.

In the Bayesian formulation of GLMs, unlike ordinary linear regression, there are no closed-form analytical solutions. One needs to specify prior probabilities for the regression coefficients. Then, their posterior probabilities are typically obtained through Monte Carlo simulations.

The arm package

In this chapter, for the purpose of illustrating Bayesian regression models, we will use the **arm** package of R. This package was developed by Andrew Gelman and co-workers, and it can be downloaded from the website at `http://CRAN.R-project.org/package=arm`.

The arm package has the `bayesglm` function that implements the Bayesian generalized linear model with an independent normal, t, or Cauchy prior distributions, for the model coefficients. We will use this function to build Bayesian regression models.

The Energy efficiency dataset

We will use the Energy efficiency dataset from the UCI Machine Learning repository for the illustration of Bayesian regression (reference 2 in the *References* section of this chapter). The dataset can be downloaded from the website at `http://archive.ics.uci.edu/ml/datasets/Energy+efficiency`. The dataset contains the measurements of energy efficiency of buildings with different building parameters. There are two energy efficiency parameters measured: heating load (*Y1*) and cooling load (*Y2*).

The building parameters used are: relative compactness (*X1*), surface area (*X2*), wall area (*X3*), roof area (*X4*), overall height (*X5*), orientation (*X6*), glazing area (*X7*), and glazing area distribution (*X8*). We will try to predict heating load as a function of all the building parameters using both ordinary regression and Bayesian regression, using the `glm` functions of the arm package. We will show that, for the same dataset, Bayesian regression gives significantly smaller prediction intervals.

Regression of energy efficiency with building parameters

In this section, we will do a linear regression of the building's energy efficiency measure, heating load (*Y1*) as a function of the building parameters. It would be useful to do a preliminary descriptive analysis to find which building variables are statistically significant. For this, we will first create bivariate plots of *Y1* and all the *X* variables. We will also compute the Spearman correlation between *Y1* and all the *X* variables.

The R script for performing these tasks is as follows:

```
>library(ggplot2)
>library(gridExtra)

>df <- read.csv("ENB2012_data.csv",header = T)
>df <- df[,c(1:9)]
>str(df)
>df[,6] <- as.numeric(df[,6])
>df[,8] <- as.numeric(df[,8])

>attach(df)
>bp1 <- ggplot(data = df,aes(x = X1,y = Y1)) + geom_point()
>bp2 <- ggplot(data = df,aes(x = X2,y = Y1)) + geom_point()
>bp3 <- ggplot(data = df,aes(x = X3,y = Y1)) + geom_point()
>bp4 <- ggplot(data = df,aes(x = X4,y = Y1)) + geom_point()
>bp5 <- ggplot(data = df,aes(x = X5,y = Y1)) + geom_point()
>bp6 <- ggplot(data = df,aes(x = X6,y = Y1)) + geom_point()
>bp7 <- ggplot(data = df,aes(x = X7,y = Y1)) + geom_point()
>bp8 <- ggplot(data = df,aes(x = X8,y = Y1)) + geom_point()
```

```
>grid.arrange(bp1,bp2,bp3,bp4,bp5,bp6,bp7,bp8,nrow = 2,ncol = 4)
>detach(df)
```

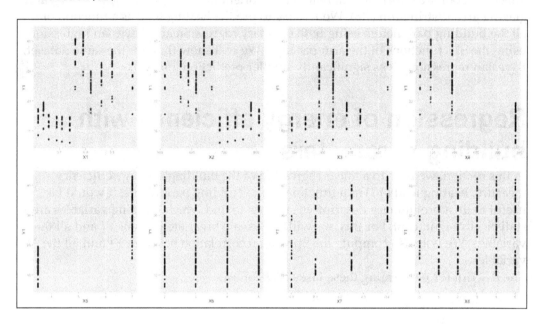

```
>cor.val <- cor(df[,1:8],df[,9],method = "spearman")
>cor.val
     [,1]
X1    0.622134697
X2  -0.622134697
X3    0.471457650
X4  -0.804027000
X5    0.861282577
X6  -0.004163071
X7    0.322860320
X8    0.068343464
```

From the b-plots and correlation coefficient values, we can conclude that variables X6 and X8 do not have a significant influence on Y1 and, hence, can be dropped from the model.

Ordinary regression

Before we look at the Bayesian linear regression, let's do an ordinary linear regression. The following R code fits the linear regression model using the lm function in the base R on the training data and predicts the values of *Y1* on the test dataset:

```
>#Removing X6 and X8 since they don't have significant correlation
with Y1
>df <- df[,c(1,2,3,4,5,7,9)]
>str(df)


>Splitting data set to Train and Test set in the ratio 80:20
>set.seed(123)
>samp <- sample.int(nrow(df),as.integer(nrow(df)*0.2),replace = F)
>dfTest <- df[samp,]
>dfTrain <- df[-samp,]
>xtest <- dfTest[,1:6]
>ytest <- dfTest[,7]


>library(arm)
>attach(dfTrain)


>#Ordinary Multivariate Regression
>fit.ols <- lm(Y1 ~ X1 + X2 + X3 + X4 + X5 + X7,data = dfTrain)
>summary(fit.ols)
>fit.coeff <- fit.ols$coefficients
>ypred.ols <- predict.lm(fit.ols,xtest,interval = "prediction",se.fit
= T)
>ypred.ols$fit
>yout.ols <- as.data.frame(cbind(ytest,ypred.ols$fit))
>ols.upr <- yout.ols$upr
>ols.lwr <- yout.ols$lwr
```

Bayesian regression

To perform Bayesian linear regression, we use the bayesglm() function of the arm package. As we described in the introduction, for the GLM, if we choose family as gaussian (the same as normal distribution) and link function as identity, then the GLM is equivalent to ordinary linear regression. Hence, if we use the bayesglm() function with the gaussian family and the identity link function, then we are performing a Bayesian linear regression.

For the Bayesian model, we need to specify a prior distribution. For the Gaussian distribution, the default settings are `prior.mean = 0`, `prior.scale = NULL`, and `prior.df = Inf`. The following R code can be used for Bayesian linear regression:

```
>fit.bayes <- bayesglm(Y1 ~ X1 + X2 + X3 + X4 + X5 + X7,family
       =gaussian(link=identity),data=dfTrain,prior.df
       = Inf,prior.mean = 0,prior.scale = NULL,maxit = 10000)
>ypred.bayes <- predict.glm(fit.bayes,newdata = xtest,se.fit = T)
>ypred.bayes$fit
```

To compare the results of the ordinary regression and Bayesian regression, we plot the prediction on test data with prediction errors for both methods on a single graph. For this purpose, we will use the **ggplot2** package:

```
>library(ggplot2)
>library(gridExtra)
>yout.ols <- as.data.frame(cbind(ytest,ypred.ols$fit))
>ols.upr <- yout.ols$upr
>ols.lwr <- yout.ols$lwr

>p.ols <- ggplot(data = yout.ols,aes(x = yout.ols$ytest,y
       = yout.ols$fit)) + geom_point()
       + ggtitle("Ordinary Regression Prediction on Test Data")
       + labs(x = "Y-Test",y = "Y-Pred")
>p.ols + geom_errorbar(ymin = ols.lwr,ymax = ols.upr)yout.bayes
       <- as.data.frame(cbind(ytest,ypred.bayes$fit))
>names(yout.bayes) <- c("ytest","fit")
>critval <- 1.96 #approx for 95% CI
>bayes.upr <- ypred.bayes$fit + critval * ypred.bayes$se.fit
>bayes.lwr <- ypred.bayes$fit - critval * ypred.bayes$se.fit

>p.bayes <- ggplot(data = yout.bayes,aes(x = yout.bayes$ytest,y
       = yout.bayes$fit)) + geom_point()
       + ggtitle("Bayesian Regression Prediction on Test Data")
       + labs(x = "Y-Test",y = "Y-Pred")
>p.bayes + geom_errorbar(ymin = bayes.lwr,ymax = bayes.upr)


>p1 <-  p.ols + geom_errorbar(ymin = ols.lwr,ymax = ols.upr)
>p2 <-  p.bayes + geom_errorbar(ymin = bayes.lwr,ymax = bayes.upr)

>grid.arrange(p1,p2,ncol = 2)
```

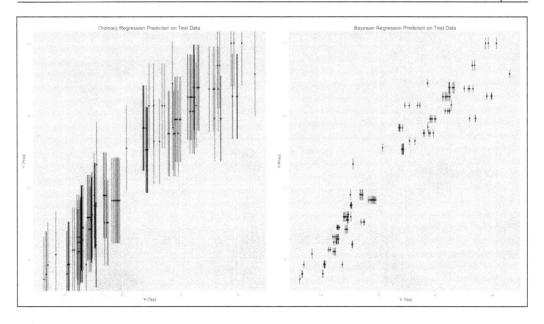

One can see that the Bayesian approach gives much more compact, 95% confident prediction intervals compared to ordinary regression. This is happening because, in the Bayesian approach, one computes a distribution of parameters. The prediction is made using a set of values sampled from the posterior distribution and averaged to get the final prediction and confidence interval.

Simulation of the posterior distribution

If one wants to find out the posterior of the model parameters, the sim( ) function of the arm package becomes handy. The following R script will simulate the posterior distribution of parameters and produce a set of histograms:

```
>posterior.bayes <- as.data.frame(coef(sim(fit.bayes)))
>attach(posterior.bayes)

>h1 <- ggplot(data = posterior.bayes,aes(x
        = X1)) + geom_histogram() + ggtitle("Histogram X1")
>h2 <- ggplot(data = posterior.bayes,aes(x
        = X2)) + geom_histogram() + ggtitle("Histogram X2")
>h3 <- ggplot(data = posterior.bayes,aes(x
        = X3)) + geom_histogram() + ggtitle("Histogram X3")
>h4 <- ggplot(data = posterior.bayes,aes(x
        = X4)) + geom_histogram() + ggtitle("Histogram X4")
```

```
>h5 <- ggplot(data = posterior.bayes,aes(x
        = X5)) + geom_histogram() + ggtitle("Histogram X5")
>h7 <- ggplot(data = posterior.bayes,aes(x
        = X7)) + geom_histogram() + ggtitle("Histogram X7")
>grid.arrange(h1,h2,h3,h4,h5,h7,nrow = 2,ncol = 3)


>detach(posterior.bayes)
```

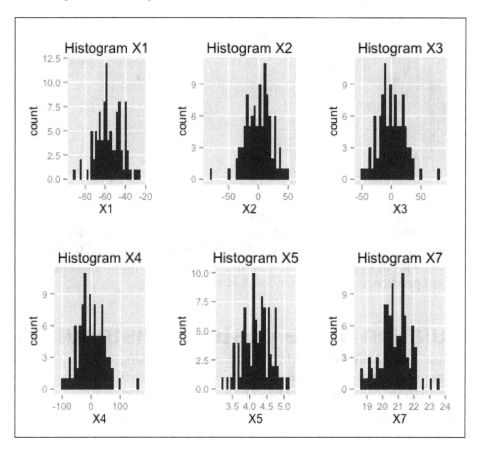

Exercises

1. Use the multivariate dataset named Auto MPG from the UCI Machine Learning repository (reference 3 in the *References* section of this chapter). The dataset can be downloaded from the website at `https://archive.ics.uci.edu/ml/datasets/Auto+MPG`. The dataset describes automobile fuel consumption in **miles per gallon** (**mpg**) for cars running in American cities. From the folder containing the datasets, download two files: `auto-mpg.data` and `auto-mpg.names`. The `auto-mpg.data` file contains the data and it is in space-separated format. The `auto-mpg.names` file has several details about the dataset, including variable names for each column. Build a regression model for the fuel efficiency, as a function displacement (*disp*), horse power (*hp*), weight (*wt*), and acceleration (*accel*), using both OLS and Bayesian GLM. Predict the values for mpg in the test dataset using both the OLS model and Bayesian GLM model (using the `bayesglm` function). Find the **Root Mean Square Error** (**RMSE**) values for OLS and Bayesian GLM and compare the accuracy and prediction intervals for both the methods.

References

1. Friedman J., Hastie T., and Tibshirani R. *The Elements of Statistical Learning – Data Mining, Inference, and Prediction*. Springer Series in Statistics. 2009

2. Tsanas A. and Xifara A. "Accurate Quantitative Estimation of Energy Performance of Residential Buildings Using Statistical Machine Learning Tools". Energy and Buildings. Vol. 49, pp. 560-567. 2012

3. Quinlan R. "Combining Instance-based and Model-based Learning". In: Tenth International Conference of Machine Learning. 236-243. University of Massachusetts, Amherst. Morgan Kaufmann. 1993. Original dataset is from StatLib library maintained by Carnegie Mellon University.

Summary

In this chapter, we illustrated how Bayesian regression is more useful for prediction with a tighter confidence interval using the Energy efficiency dataset and the `bayesglm` function of the arm package. We also learned how to simulate the posterior distribution using the `sim` function in the same R package. In the next chapter, we will learn about Bayesian classification.

6
Bayesian Classification Models

We introduced the classification machine learning task in *Chapter 4, Machine Learning Using Bayesian Inference*, and said that the objective of classification is to assign a data record into one of the predetermined classes. Classification is one of the most studied machine learning tasks and there are several well-established state of the art methods for it. These include logistic regression models, support vector machines, random forest models, and neural network models. With sufficient labeled training data, these models can achieve accuracies above 95% in many practical problems.

Then, the obvious question is, why would you need to use Bayesian methods for classification? There are two answers to this question. One is that often it is difficult to get a large amount of labeled data for training. When there are hundreds or thousands of features in a given problem, one often needs a large amount of training data for these supervised methods to avoid overfitting. Bayesian methods can overcome this problem through Bayesian averaging and hence require only a small to medium size training data. Secondly, most of the methods, such as SVM or NN, are like black box machines. They will give you very accurate results, but little insight as to which variables are important for the example. Often, in many practical problems, for example, in the diagnosis of a disease, it is important to identify leading causes. Therefore, a black box approach would not be sufficient. Bayesian methods have an inherent feature called **Automatic Relevance Determination** (**ARD**) by which important variables in a problem can be identified.

In this chapter, two Bayesian classification models will be discussed. The first one is the popular Naïve Bayes method for text classification. The second is the Bayesian logistic regression model. Before we discuss each of these models, let's review some of the performance metrics that are commonly used in the classification task.

Performance metrics for classification

To understand the concepts easily, let's take the case of binary classification, where the task is to classify an input feature vector into one of the two states: -1 or 1. Assume that 1 is the positive class and -1 is the negative class. The predicted output contains only -1 or 1, but there can be two types of errors. Some of the -1 in the test set could be predicted as 1. This is called a **false positive or type I** error. Similarly, some of the 1 in the test set could be predicted as -1. This is called a **false negative or type II** error. These two types of errors can be represented in the case of binary classification as a confusion matrix as shown below.

Confusion Matrix		Predicted Class	
		Positive	Negative
Actual Class	Positive	TP	FN
	Negative	FP	TN

From the confusion matrix, we can derive the following performance metrics:

- **Precision**: $Pr = \frac{TP}{(TP + FP)}$ This gives the percentage of correct answers in the output predicted as positive

- **Recall**: $Re = \frac{TP}{(TP + FP)}$ This gives the percentage of positives in the test data set that have been correctly predicted

- **F-Score**: $F = \frac{2\ Pr\ Rs}{(Pr + Rs)}$ This is the geometric mean of precision and recall

- **True positive rate**: $Tpr = \frac{TP}{P}$ This is the same as recall

- **False positive rate**: $Fpr = \frac{FP}{N}$ This gives the percentage of negative classes classified as positive

Also, *Tpr* is called *sensitivity* and *1 - Fpr* is called *specificity* of the classifier. A plot of Tpr versus Fpr (*sensitivity* versus *1 - specificity*) is called an **ROC** curve (it stands for **receiver operating characteristic** curve). This is used to find the best threshold (operating point of the classifier) for deciding whether a predicted output (usually a score or probability) belongs to class 1 or -1.

Usually, the threshold is taken as the inflation point of the ROC curve that gives the best performance with the least false predictions. The area under the ROC curve or AUC is another measure of classifier performance. For a purely random model, the ROC curve will be a straight line along the diagonal. The corresponding value of AUC will be 0.5. Classifiers with AUC above 0.8 will be considered as good, though this very much depends on the problem to be solved.

The Naïve Bayes classifier

The name Naïve Bayes comes from the basic assumption in the model that the probability of a particular feature X_i is independent of any other feature X_j given the class label C_k. This implies the following:

$$P\left(X_i \mid C_k, X_j\right) = P\left(X_i \mid C_k\right)$$

Using this assumption and the Bayes rule, one can show that the probability of class C_k, given features $\{X_1, X_2, \cdots, X_n\}$, is given by:

$$P\left(C_k \mid \{X_1, X_2, \cdots, X_n\}\right) = \frac{1}{P\left(X_1, X_2, \cdots, X_n\right)} P\left(C_k\right) \prod_{i=1}^{N} P\left(X_i \mid C_k\right)$$

Here, $P(X_1, X_2, \cdots, X_n)$ is the normalization term obtained by summing the numerator on all the values of k. It is also called Bayesian evidence or partition function Z. The classifier selects a class label as the target class that maximizes the posterior class probability $P\left(C_k \mid \{X_1, X_2, \cdots, X_n\}\right)$:

$$\hat{C} = \underset{k \in \{C_1, C_2, \cdots C_K\}}{\operatorname{argmax}} P\left(C_k\right) \prod_{i=1}^{N} P\left(X_i \mid C_k\right)$$

The Naïve Bayes classifier is a baseline classifier for document classification. One reason for this is that the underlying assumption that each feature (words or m-grams) is independent of others, given the class label typically holds good for text. Another reason is that the Naïve Bayes classifier scales well when there is a large number of documents.

There are two implementations of Naïve Bayes. In Bernoulli Naïve Bayes, features are binary variables that encode whether a feature (m-gram) is present or absent in a document. In multinomial Naïve Bayes, the features are frequencies of m-grams in a document. To avoid issues when the frequency is zero, a Laplace smoothing is done on the feature vectors by adding a 1 to each count. Let's look at multinomial Naïve Bayes in some detail.

Let n_i be the number of times the feature X_i occurred in the class C_K in the training data. Then, the likelihood function of observing a feature vector $X = \{X_1, X_2, \cdots, X_n\}$, given a class label C_K, is given by:

$$P(X \mid C_K) = \frac{(\sum_i n_i)!}{(\prod_i n_i)!} \prod_i p_{k_i}^{n_i}$$

Here, p_{k_i} is the probability of observing the feature X_i in the class C_K.

Using Bayesian rule, the posterior probability of observing the class C_K, given a feature vector X, is given by:

$$P(C_K \mid X) = \frac{1}{2} P(C_K) \prod_i p_{k_i}^{n_i}$$

Taking logarithm on both the sides and ignoring the constant term Z, we get the following:

$$\log P(C_K \mid X) = \log P(C_K) + \sum_i \left(\log p_{k_i}\right) n_i$$

So, by taking logarithm of posterior distribution, we have converted the problem into a linear regression model with $b_i = \log p_{k_i}$ as the coefficients to be determined from data. This can be easily solved. Generally, instead of term frequencies, one uses TF-IDF (term frequency multiplied by inverse frequency) with the document length normalized to improve the performance of the model.

The R package **e1071** (*Miscellaneous Functions of the Department of Statistics*) by T.U. Wien contains an R implementation of Naïve Bayes. For this chapter, we will use the SMS spam dataset from the UCI Machine Learning repository (reference 1 in the *References* section of this chapter). The dataset consists of 425 SMS spam messages collected from the UK forum Grumbletext, where consumers can submit spam SMS messages. The dataset also contains 3375 normal (ham) SMS messages from the NUS SMS corpus maintained by the National University of Singapore.

The dataset can be downloaded from the UCI Machine Learning repository (https://archive.ics.uci.edu/ml/datasets/SMS+Spam+Collection). Let's say that we have saved this as file SMSSpamCollection.txt in the working directory of R (actually, you need to open it in Excel and save it is as tab-delimited file for it to read in R properly).

Then, the command to read the file into the tm (text mining) package would be the following:

```
>spamdata <-read.table("SMSSpamCollection.txt",sep="\
t",stringsAsFactors = default.stringsAsFactors())
```

We will first separate the dependent variable y and independent variables x and split the dataset into training and testing sets in the ratio 80:20, using the following R commands:

```
>samp<-sample.int(nrow(spamdata),as.integer(nrow(spamdata)*0.2),repla
ce=F)
>spamTest <-spamdata[samp,]
>spamTrain <-spamdata[-samp,]
>ytrain<-as.factor(spamTrain[,1])
>ytest<-as.factor(spamTest[,1])
>xtrain<-as.vector(spamTrain[,2])
>xtest<-as.vector(spamTest[,2])
```

Since we are dealing with text documents, we need to do some standard preprocessing before we can use the data for any machine learning models. We can use the tm package in R for this purpose. In the next section, we will describe this in some detail.

Text processing using the tm package

The **tm** package has methods for data import, corpus handling, preprocessing, metadata management, and creation of term-document matrices. Data can be imported into the tm package either from a directory, a vector with each component a document, or a data frame. The fundamental data structure in tm is an abstract collection of text documents called Corpus. It has two implementations; one is where data is stored in memory and is called **VCorpus (volatile corpus)** and the second is where data is stored in the hard disk and is called **PCorpus (permanent corpus)**.

We can create a corpus of our SMS spam dataset by using the following R commands; prior to this, you need to install the tm package and **SnowballC** package by using the install.packages("packagename") command in R:

```
>library(tm)
>library(SnowballC)
>xtrain <- VCorpus(VectorSource(xtrain))
```

First, we need to do some basic text processing, such as removing extra white space, changing all words to lowercase, removing stop words, and stemming the words. This can be achieved by using the following functions in the tm package:

```
>#remove extra white space
>xtrain <- tm_map(xtrain,stripWhitespace)
>#remove punctuation
>xtrain <- tm_map(xtrain,removePunctuation)
>#remove numbers
>xtrain <- tm_map(xtrain,removeNumbers)
>#changing to lower case
>xtrain <- tm_map(xtrain,content_transformer(tolower))
>#removing stop words
>xtrain <- tm_map(xtrain,removeWords,stopwords("english"))
>#stemming the document
>xtrain <- tm_map(xtrain,stemDocument)
```

Finally, the data is transformed into a form that can be consumed by machine learning models. This is the so called document-term matrix form where each document (SMS in this case) is a row, the terms appearing in all documents are the columns, and the entry in each cell denotes how many times each word occurs in one document:

```
>#creating Document-Term Matrix
>xtrain <- as.data.frame.matrix(DocumentTermMatrix(xtrain))
```

The same set of processes is done on the `xtest` dataset as well. The reason we converted *y* to factors and *xtrain* to a data frame is to match the input format for the Naïve Bayes classifier in the e1071 package.

Model training and prediction

You need to first install the e1071 package from CRAN. The `naiveBayes()` function can be used to train the Naïve Bayes model. The function can be called using two methods. The following is the first method:

```
>naiveBayes(formula,data,laplace=0,…,subset,na.action=na.pass)
```

Here `formula` stands for the linear combination of independent variables to predict the following class:

```
>class ~ x1+x2+…
```

Also, `data` stands for either a data frame or contingency table consisting of categorical and numerical variables.

If we have the class labels as a vector y and dependent variables as a data frame x, then we can use the second method of calling the function, as follows:

```
>naiveBayes(x,y,laplace=0,…)
```

We will use the second method of calling in our example. Once we have a trained model, which is an R object of class `naiveBayes`, we can predict the classes of new instances as follows:

```
>predict(object,newdata,type=c(class,raw),threshold=0.001,eps=0,…)
```

So, we can train the Naïve Bayes model on our training dataset and score on the test dataset by using the following commands:

```
>#Training the Naive Bayes Model
>nbmodel <- naiveBayes(xtrain,ytrain,laplace=3)
>#Prediction using trained model
>ypred.nb <- predict(nbmodel,xtest,type = "class",threshold = 0.075)
>#Converting classes to 0 and 1 for plotting ROC
>fconvert <- function(x){
    if(x == "spam"){ y <- 1}
  else {y <- 0}
  y
}

>ytest1 <- sapply(ytest,fconvert,simplify = "array")
>ypred1 <- sapply(ypred.nb,fconvert,simplify = "array")
>roc(ytest1,ypred1,plot = T)
```

Here, the ROC curve for this model and dataset is shown. This is generated using the pROC package in CRAN:

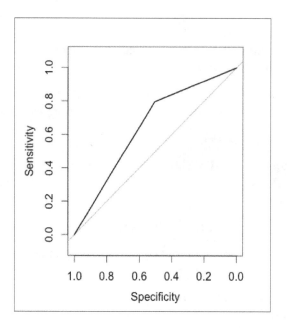

```
>#Confusion matrix
>confmat <- table(ytest,ypred.nb)
>confmat
pred.nb
ytest   ham spam
   ham  143  139
   spam   9   35
```

From the ROC curve and confusion matrix, one can choose the best threshold for the classifier, and the precision and recall metrics. Note that the example shown here is for illustration purposes only. The model needs be to tuned further to improve accuracy.

We can also print some of the most frequent words (model features) occurring in the two classes and their posterior probabilities generated by the model. This will give a more intuitive feeling for the model exercise. The following R code does this job:

```
>tab <- nbmodel$tables
>fham <- function(x){
  y <- x[1,1]
```

```
      y
}
>hamvec <- sapply(tab,fham,simplify = "array")
>hamvec <- sort(hamvec,decreasing = T)

>fspam <- function(x){
  y <- x[2,1]
  y
}
>spamvec <- sapply(tab,fspam,simplify = "array")
>spamvec <- sort(spamvec,decreasing = T)
>prb <- cbind(spamvec,hamvec)
>print.table(prb)
```

The output table is as follows:

word	Prob(word | spam)	Prob(word | ham)
call	0.6994	0.4084
free	0.4294	0.3996
now	0.3865	0.3120
repli	0.2761	0.3094
text	0.2638	0.2840
spam	0.2270	0.2726
txt	0.2270	0.2594
get	0.2209	0.2182
stop	0.2086	0.2025

The table shows, for example, that given a document is spam, the probability of the word *call* appearing in it is 0.6994, whereas the probability of the same word appearing in a normal document is only 0.4084.

The Bayesian logistic regression model

The name logistic regression comes from the fact that the dependent variable of the regression is a logistic function. It is one of the widely used models in problems where the response is a binary variable (for example, fraud or not-fraud, click or no-click, and so on).

A logistic function is defined by the following equation:

$$\sigma(Y) = \frac{e^Y}{e^Y + 1} = \frac{1}{1 + e^{-Y}}$$

It has the particular feature that, as y varies from $-\infty$ to $+\infty$, the function value varies from 0 to 1. Hence, the logistic function is ideal for modeling any binary response as the input signal is varied.

The inverse of the logistic function is called *logit*. It is defined as follows:

$$g(\sigma(Y)) = \ln\left[\frac{\sigma(Y)}{1 - \sigma(Y)}\right] = Y$$

In logistic regression, y is treated as a linear function of explanatory variables X. Therefore, the logistic regression model can be defined as follows:

$$\ln\left[\frac{\sigma(Y)}{1 - \sigma(Y)}\right] = \theta_1 b_1(X) + \theta_2 b_2(X) + \cdots + \theta_M b_M(X)$$

Here, $\{b_i(X)\}$ is the set of basis functions and $\{\theta_i\}$ are the model parameters as explained in the case of linear regression in *Chapter 4, Machine Learning Using Bayesian Inference*. From the definition of GLM in *Chapter 5, Bayesian Regression Models*, one can immediately recognize that logistic regression is a special case of GLM with the **logit** function as the link function.

Bayesian treatment of logistic regression is more difficult compared to the case of linear regression. Here, the likelihood function consists of a product of logistic functions; one for each data point. To compute the posterior, one has to normalize this function multiplied by the prior (to get the denominator of the Bayes formula). One approach is to use Laplace approximation as explained in *Chapter 3, Introducing Bayesian Inference*. Readers might recall that in Laplace approximation, the posterior is approximated as a Gaussian (normal) distribution about the maximum of the posterior. This is achieved by finding the **maximum a posteriori** (**MAP**) solution first and computing the second derivative of the negative log likelihood around the MAP solution. Interested readers can find the details of Laplace approximation to logistic regression in the paper by D.J.C. MacKay (reference 2 in the *References* section of this chapter).

Instead of using an analytical approximation, Polson and Scott recently proposed a fully Bayesian treatment of this problem using a data augmentation strategy (reference 3 in the *References* section of this chapter). The authors have implemented their method in the R package: BayesLogit. We will use this package to illustrate Bayesian logistic regression in this chapter.

The BayesLogit R package

The package can be downloaded from the CRAN website at http://cran.r-project.org/web/packages/BayesLogit/index.html. The package contains the logit function that can be used to perform a Bayesian logistic regression. The syntax for calling this function is as follows:

```
>logit(Y,X,n=rep(1,length(Y) ),m0=rep(0,ncol(X) ),P0
         =matrix(0,nrow=ncol(X),ncol=ncol(X) ),samp=1000,burn
         =500)
```

Here, Y is an N-dimensional vector containing response values; X is an $N \times P$ dimensional matrix containing values of independent variables, n is an N-dimensional vector, m_0 is a P-dimensional prior mean, and P_0 is a $P \times P$ dimensional prior precision. The other two arguments are related to MCMC simulation parameters. The number of MCMC simulations saved is denoted by samp and the number of MCMC simulations discarded at the beginning of the run before saving samples is denoted by burn.

The dataset

To illustrate Bayesian logistic regression, we use the Parkinsons dataset from the UCI Machine Learning repository (https://archive.ics.uci.edu/ml/datasets/Parkinsons). The dataset was used by Little et.al. to detect Parkinson's disease by analyzing voice disorder (reference 4 in the *References* section of this chapter). The dataset consists of voice measurements from 31 people, of which 23 people have Parkinson's disease. There are 195 rows corresponding to multiple measurements from a single individual. The measurements can be grouped into the following sets:

- The vocal fundamental frequency
- Jitter
- Shimmer
- The ratio of noise to tonal components

- The nonlinear dynamical complexity measures
- The signal fractal scaling exponent
- The nonlinear measures of fundamental frequency variation

In total, there are 22 numerical attributes.

Preparation of the training and testing datasets

Before we can train the Bayesian logistic model, we need to do some preprocessing of the data. The dataset contains multiple measurements from the same individual. Here, we take all observations; each from a sampled set of individuals in order to create the training and test sets. Also, we need to separate the dependent variable (class label Y) from the independent variables (X). The following R code does this job:

```
>#install.packages("BayesLogit") #One time installation of package
>library(BayesLogit)
>PDdata <- read.table("parkinsons.csv",sep=",",
header=TRUE,row.names = 1)
>rnames <- row.names(PDdata)
>cnames <- colnames(PDdata,do.NULL = TRUE,prefix = "col")
>colnames(PDdata)[17] <- "y"
>PDdata$y <- as.factor(PDdata$y)

>rnames.strip <- substr(rnames,10,12)
>PDdata1 <- cbind(PDdata,rnames.strip)
>rnames.unique <- unique(rnames.strip)
>set.seed(123)
>samp <- sample(rnames.unique,as.integer(length(rnames.unique)
        *0.2),replace=F)
>PDtest <- PDdata1[PDdata1$rnames.strip %in% samp,-24]   #
        -24 to remove last column
>PDtrain <- PDdata1[!(PDdata1$rnames.strip %in% samp),-24] #
        -24 to remove last column
>xtrain <- PDtrain[,-17]
>ytrain <- PDtrain[,17]
>xtest <- PDtest[,-17]
>ytest<- PDtest[,17]
```

Using the Bayesian logistic model

We can use *xtrain* and *ytrain* to train the Bayesian logistic regression model using the `logit( )` function:

```
>blmodel <- logit(ytrain,xtrain,n=rep(1,length(ytrain)),m0
        = rep(0,ncol(xtrain)),P0 = matrix(0,nrow
        =ncol(xtrain),ncol=ncol(xtrain)),samp = 1000,burn = 500)
```

The `summary( )` function will give a high-level summary of the fitted model:

```
>summary(blmodel)
```

To predict values of *Y* for a new dataset, we need to write a custom script as follows:

```
>psi <- blmodel$beta %*% t(xtrain)   # samp x n
>p   <- exp(psi) / (1 + exp(psi) )   # samp x n
>ypred.bayes <- colMeans(p)
```

The error of prediction can be computed by comparing it with the actual values of *Y* present in *ytest*:

```
>table(ypred.bayes,ytest)
```

One can plot the ROC curve using the pROC package as follows:

```
>roc(ytrain,ypred.bayes,plot = T)
```

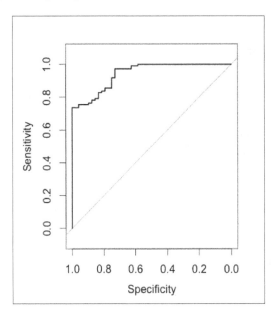

The ROC curve has an AUC of 0.942 suggesting a good classification accuracy. Again, the model is presented here to illustrate the purpose and is not tuned to obtain maximum performance.

Exercises

1. In this exercise, we will use the DBWorld e-mails dataset from the UCI Machine Learning repository to compare the relative performance of Naïve Bayes and BayesLogit methods. The dataset contains 64 e-mails from the DBWorld newsletter and the task is to classify the e-mails into either *announcements of conferences* or *everything else*. The reference for this dataset is a course by Prof. Michele Filannino (reference 5 in the *References* section of this chapter). The dataset can be downloaded from the UCI website at `https://archive.ics.uci.edu/ml/datasets/DBWorld+e-mails#`.

    Some preprocessing of the dataset would be required to use it for both the methods. The dataset is in the ARFF format. You need to download the **foreign** R package (`http://cran.r-project.org/web/packages/foreign/index.html`) and use the `read.arff( )` method in it to read the file into an R data frame.

References

1. Almeida T.A., Gómez Hidalgo J.M., and Yamakami A. "Contributions to the Study of SMS Spam Filtering: New Collection and Results". In: 2011 ACM Symposium on Document Engineering (DOCENG'11). Mountain View, CA, USA. 2011

2. MacKay D.J.C. "The Evidence Framework Applied to Classification Networks". Neural Computation 4(5)

3. "Bayesian Inference for Logistic Models Using Pólya-Gamma Latent Variables". Journal of the American Statistical Association. Volume 108, Issue 504, Page 1339. 2013

4. Costello D.A.E., Little M.A., McSharry P.E., Moroz I.M., and Roberts S.J. "Exploiting Nonlinear Recurrence and Fractal Scaling Properties for Voice Disorder Detection". BioMedical Engineering OnLine. 2007

5. Filannino M. "DBWorld e-mail Classification Using a Very Small Corpus". Project of Machine Learning Course. University of Manchester. 2011

Summary

In this chapter, we discussed the various merits of using Bayesian inference for the classification task. We reviewed some of the common performance metrics used for the classification task. We also learned two basic and popular methods for classification, Naïve Bayes and logistic regression, both implemented using the Bayesian approach. Having learned some important Bayesian-supervised machine learning techniques, in the next chapter, we will discuss some unsupervised Bayesian models.

7
Bayesian Models for Unsupervised Learning

The machine learning models that we have discussed so far in the previous two chapters share one common characteristic: they require training data containing ground truth. This implies a dataset containing true values of the predicate or dependent variable that is often manually labeled. Such machine learning where the algorithm is trained using labeled data is called **supervised learning**. This type of machine learning gives a very good performance in terms of accuracy of prediction. It is, in fact, the de facto method used in most industrial systems using machine learning. However, the drawback of this method is that, when one wants to train a model with large datasets, it would be difficult to get the labeled data. This is particularly relevant in the era of Big Data as a lot of data is available for organizations from various logs, transactions, and interactions with consumers; organizations want to gain insight from this data and make predictions about their consumers' interests.

In unsupervised methods, no labeled data is required for learning. The process of learning happens through identifying dominant patterns and correlations present in the dataset. Some common examples of unsupervised learning are clustering, association rule mining, density estimation, and dimensional reduction. In clustering, naturally occurring groups in data are identified using a suitable algorithm that makes use of some distance measure between data points. In association rule mining, items that frequently occur together in a transaction are identified from a transaction dataset. In dimensional reduction techniques such as principal component analysis, the original dataset containing a large number of variables (dimensions) is projected down to a lower dimensional space where the maximum information in the data is present. Though unsupervised learning doesn't require labeled training data, one would need a large amount of data to learn all the patterns of interest and often the learning is more computationally intensive.

In many practical cases, it would be feasible to create a small amount of labeled data. The third type of learning, semi-supervised learning, is a method that makes use of this small labeled dataset and propagates labels to the rest of the unlabeled training data using suitable algorithms. In this chapter, we will cover Bayesian approaches for unsupervised learnings. We will discuss in detail two important models: Gaussian mixture models for clustering and Latent Dirichlet allocation for topic modeling.

Bayesian mixture models

In general, a mixture model corresponds to representing data using a mixture of probability distributions. The most common mixture model is of the following type:

$$P(X) = \sum_{k=1}^{K} \pi_k P(X; \Theta_k)$$

Here, $P(X;\Theta_k)$ is a probability distribution of X with parameters Θ_k, and π_k represents the weight for the kth component in the mixture, such that $\sum_{k=1}^{K} \pi_k = 1$. If the underlying probability distribution is a normal (Gaussian) distribution, then the mixture model is called a **Gaussian mixture model** (**GMM**). The mathematical representation of GMM, therefore, is given by:

$$P(X) = \sum_{k=1}^{K} \pi_k N(X; \mu_k, \Sigma_k)$$

Here, we have used the same notation, as in previous chapters, where X stands for an N-dimensional data vector $X = \{x_1, x_2, \cdots, x_N\}$ representing each observation and there are M such observations in the dataset.

A mixture model such as this is suitable for clustering when the clusters have overlaps. One of the applications of GMM is in computer vision. If one wants to track moving objects in a video, it is useful to subtract the background image. This is called background subtraction or foreground detection. GMMs are used for this purpose where the intensity of each pixel is modeled using a mixture of Gaussian distributions (reference 1 in the *References* section of this chapter).

The task of learning GMMs corresponds to learning the model parameters $\Theta_k = (\mu_k, \Sigma_k)$ and mixture weights π_k for all the components $(k = 1, \cdots, K)$. The standard approach for learning GMMs is by using the **maximum likelihood** method. For a dataset consisting of M observations, the logarithm of the likelihood function is given by:

$$\ln P(X; \pi, \mu, \Sigma) = \sum_{i=1}^{M} \ln \left(\sum_{k=1}^{K} \pi_k N(X_i; \mu_k, \Sigma_k) \right)$$

Unlike a single Gaussian model, maximizing the log-likelihood with respect to parameters π, μ, Σ cannot be done in a straightforward manner in GMM. This is because there is no closed-form expression for the derivative in this case, since it is difficult to compute the logarithm of a sum. Therefore, one uses what is called an **expectation-maximization (EM)** algorithm to maximize the log-likelihood function. The EM algorithm is an iterative algorithm, where each iteration consists of two computations: expectation and maximization. The EM algorithm proceeds as follows:

1. Initialize parameters μ_k, Σ_k, and π_k and evaluate the initial value of log-likelihood.

2. In the expectation step, evaluate mixture components π_k from log-likelihood using the current parameter values μ_k and Σ_k.

3. In the maximization step, using the values of π_k computed in step 2, estimate new parameter values μ_k and Σ_k by the maximization of log-likelihood.

4. Compute a new value of the log-likelihood function using the estimated values of π_k, μ_k, and Σ_k from steps 2 and 3.

5. Repeat steps 2-4 until the log-likelihood function is converged.

In the Bayesian treatment of GMM, the maximization of log-likelihood is simplified by introducing a latent variable Z. Let Z be a K-dimensional binary random variable having only one element 1, and the rest of the $K - 1$ elements are 0. Using Z, one can write the joint distribution of X and Z as follows:

$$P(X, Z) \quad P(X | Z) P(Z)$$

Here:

$$P(Z) = \prod_{k=1}^{K} (\pi_k)^{Z_k}$$

And:

$$P(X \mid Z) = \prod_{k=1}^{K} \left(N\left(X; \boldsymbol{\mu}_k, \Sigma_k\right) \right)^{Z_k}$$

Therefore:

$$P(X) = \sum_{Z} P(X \mid Z) P(Z) = \sum_{k=1}^{K} \pi_k N\left(X; \boldsymbol{\mu}_k, \Sigma_k\right)$$

And:

$$P(X, Z) = \prod_{m=1}^{M} \prod_{k=1}^{K} \left(\pi_k\right)^{Z_{mk}} \left(N\left(X; \boldsymbol{\mu}_k, \Sigma_k\right) \right)^{Z_{mk}}$$

The advantage of introducing a latent variable Z in the problem is that the expression for log-likelihood is simplified, where the logarithm directly acts on the normal distribution as in the case of a single Gaussian model. Therefore, it is straightforward to maximize $P(X, Z)$. However, the problem that still remains is that we don't know the value of Z! So, the trick is to use an EM-like iterative algorithm where, in the E-step, the expectation value of Z is estimated and in the M-step, using the last estimated value of Z, we find the parameter values of the Gaussian distribution. The Bayesian version of the EM algorithm for GMM proceeds as follows:

1. Initialize parameters μ_k, Σ_k, and π_k and evaluate the initial value of log-likelihood.

2. In the expectation step, use these values to compute the expectation value $\left(Z_{mk}\right)$.

3. In the maximization step, using (Z_{mk}) fixed, estimate μ_k and Σ_k by maximizing $\log P(X, Z)$.

4. Compute the new likelihood function.

5. Repeat steps 2-4 until convergence.

A more detailed treatment of the Bayesian version of the EM algorithm and GMM can be found in the book by Christopher M. Bishop (reference 2 in the *References* section of this chapter). Here, we leave the theoretical treatment of the Bayesian GMM and proceed to look at its R implementation in the **bgmm** package.

The bgmm package for Bayesian mixture models

The bgmm package was developed by Przemyslaw Biecek and Ewa Szczurek for modeling gene expressions data (reference 3 in the *References* section of this chapter). It can be downloaded from the CRAN website at `http://cran.r-project.org/web/packages/bgmm/index.html`. The package contains not only an unsupervised version of GMM but fully supervised and semi-supervised implementations as well. The following are the different models available in the bgmm package:

- **Fully supervised GMM**: This is the labeled data available for all records in a training set. This includes the following:

    ° The `supervised( )` function

- **Semi-supervised GMM**: This is the labeled data available for a small subset of all records in a training set. This includes the following

    ° The `semisupervised( )` function

- **Partially supervised GMM**: This is the labeled data available for a small subset of all records, but these labels are uncertain. The values of labels are given with some probability. There are two functions in the package for partially supervised GMM. This includes the following::

    ° The `belief( )` function: The uncertainty of labels is expressed as a probability distribution over its components. For the first m observations, a belief matrix B of dimensions $m \times k$ is given as input where the matrix entry b_{ij} denotes the probability that the ith record has the jth label.

    ° The `soft( )` function: In this approach, a plausibility matrix of dimension $M \times k$ is defined across all records in the training set of size M. The matrix element p_{ij} is interpreted as the weight of the prior probability that the ith record has the jth label. If there is no particular information about labels of any records, they can be given equal weights. For the purpose of implementation, a constraint is imposed on the matrix elements: $\sum_{j=1}^{k} p_{ij} = 1$.

- **Unsupervised GMM**: This labeled data is not available for any records. This includes the following:

    ° The `unsupervised( )` function

The typical parameters that are passed to these functions are as follows:

- X: This is a data.frame with the unlabelled X data.
- *knowns*: This is a data.frame with the labeled X data.
- B: This is a belief matrix that specifies the distribution of beliefs for the labeled records. The number of rows of B should be the same as that of *knowns*.
- P: This is a matrix of weights of prior probabilities (plausibilities).
- *class*: This is a vector of classes or labels for the labeled records.
- k: This is the number of components or columns of the B matrix.
- *init.params*: These are the initial values for the estimates of model parameters.

The difference between the `belief( )` and `soft( )` functions is that, in the first case, the input is a matrix containing prior probability values for each possible label, whereas in the second case, the input is a matrix containing weights for each of the priors and not the prior probability itself. For more details, readers are requested to read the paper by Przemyslaw Biecek et.al (reference 3 in the *References* section of this chapter).

Now, let's do a small illustrative example of using bgmm. We will use the ADL dataset from the UCI Machine Learning repository. This dataset contains acceleration data from wrist-worn accelerometers from 16 volunteers. The dataset and metadata details can be found at `https://archive.ics.uci.edu/ml/datasets/Dataset+for+AD L+Recognition+with+Wrist-worn+Accelerometer`. The research work on ADL monitoring systems, where this dataset was generated, is published in the two papers by Bruno B. et.al. (reference 4 and reference 5 in the *References* section of this chapter).

For the example of bgmm, we will only use one folder in the dataset directory, namely `Brush_teeth`. Firstly, we will do a small amount of preprocessing to combine data from the different volunteers into a single file. The following R script does this job:

```
>#Set working directory to folder containing files (provide the
correct path)
>setwd("C:/…/ADL_Dataset/HMP_Dataset/Brush_teeth")
>flist <- list.files(path
          = "C:/../ADL_Dataset/HMP_Dataset/Brush_teeth",pattern
          = "*.txt")
>all.data <- lapply(flist,read.table,sep = " ",header = FALSE)
>combined.data <- as.data.frame(do.call(rbind,all.data))
>combined.data.XZ <- combined.data[,c(1,3)]
```

The last step is to select the X and Z components of acceleration to create a two-dimensional dataset.

The following R script calls the `bgmm` function and performs clustering. A simple scatter plot of the data suggests that there could be four clusters in the dataset and choosing *k = 4* would be sufficient:

```
>modelbgmm <- unsupervised(combined.data.XZ,k=4)
>summary(modelbgmm)
>plot.mModel(modelbgmm)
```

The clusters generated by bgmm can be seen in the following figure; there are four clusters whose centers are represented by the four color dots and their respective Gaussian densities are represented by the ellipses:

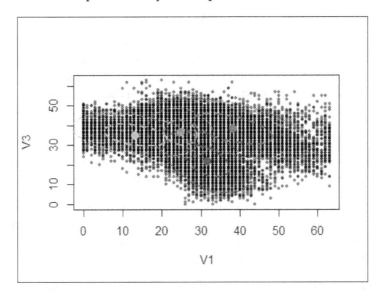

Topic modeling using Bayesian inference

We have seen the supervised learning (classification) of text documents in *Chapter 6, Bayesian Classification Models*, using the Naïve Bayes model. Often, a large text document, such as a news article or a short story, can contain different topics as subsections. It is useful to model such intra-document statistical correlations for the purpose of classification, summarization, compression, and so on. The Gaussian mixture model learned in the previous section is more applicable for numerical data, such as images, and not for documents. This is because words in documents seldom follow normal distribution. A more appropriate choice would be multinomial distribution.

A powerful extension of mixture models to documents is the work of T. Hofmann on Probabilistic Semantic Indexing (reference 6 in the *References* section of this chapter) and that of David Blei, et. al. on Latent Dirichlet allocation (reference 7 in the *References* section of this chapter). In these works, a document is described as a mixture of topics and each topic is described by a distribution of words. LDA is a generative unsupervised model for text documents. The task of LDA is to learn the parameters of the topic distribution, word distributions, and mixture coefficients from data. A brief overview of LDA is presented in the next section. Readers are strongly advised to read the paper by David Blei, et al. to comprehend their approach.

Latent Dirichlet allocation

In LDA, it is assumed that words are the basic units of documents. A word is one element of a set known as vocabulary, indexed by $\{1, \cdots, V\}$. Here, V denotes the size of the vocabulary. A word can be represented by a unit-basis vector, whose all components are zero except the one corresponding to the word that has a value 1. For example, the nth word in a vocabulary is described by a vector of size V, whose n^{th} component $w^n = 1$ and all other components $w^m = 0$ for $m \neq n$. Similarly, a document is a collection of N words denoted by $w = \{w_1, w_2, \cdots, w_N\}$ and a corpus is a collection of M documents denoted by $D = (w_1, w_2, \cdots, w_M)$ (note that documents are represented here by a bold face **w**, whereas words are without bold face w).

As mentioned earlier, LDA is a generative probabilistic model of a corpus where documents are represented as random mixtures over latent topics and each topic is characterized by a distribution over words. To generate each document **w** in a corpus in an LDA model, the following steps are performed:

1. Choose the value of N corresponding to the size of the document, according to a Poisson distribution characterized by parameter ξ:

$$N \sim Poisson(\xi)$$

2. Choose the value of parameter Θ that characterizes the topic distribution from a Dirichlet distribution characterized by parameter α:

$$\Theta \sim Dir(\alpha)$$

3. For each of the N words w_n :

   1. Choose a topic z_n according to the multinomial distribution characterized by the parameter Θ drawn in step 2:

   $$z_n \sim Multinominal(\Theta)$$

   2. Choose a word w_n : from the multinomial probability distribution characterized by β and conditioned on z_n :

   $$w_n \sim p(w_n \mid z_n, \beta)$$

Given values of N, α, and β, the joint distribution of a topic mixture Θ, set of topics **z**, and set of words **w**, is given by:

$$p(\Theta, z, w \mid \alpha, \beta) = p(\Theta \mid \alpha) \prod_{i=1}^{N} p(z_n \mid \Theta) p(w_n \mid z_n, \beta)$$

Note that, in this case, only w is observed (the documents) and both Θ and **z** are treated as latent (hidden) variables.

The Bayesian inference problem in LDA is the estimation of the posterior density of latent variables Θ and **z**, given a document given by:

$$p(\Theta, z \mid w, \alpha, \beta) = \frac{p(\Theta, z, w \mid \alpha, \beta)}{p(w \mid \alpha, \beta)}$$

As usual, with many Bayesian models, this is intractable analytically and one has to use approximate techniques, such as MCMC or variational Bayes, to estimate the posterior.

R packages for LDA

There are mainly two packages in R that can be used for performing LDA on documents. One is the **topicmodels** package developed by Bettina Grün and Kurt Hornik and the second one is **lda** developed by Jonathan Chang. Here, we describe both these packages.

The topicmodels package

The topicmodels package is an interface to the C and C++ codes developed by the authors of the papers on LDA and **Correlated Topic Models (CTM)** (references 7, 8, and 9 in the *References* section of this chapter). The main function LDA in this package is used to fit LDA models. It can be called by:

```
>LDA(X,K,method = "Gibbs",control = NULL,model = NULL,...)
```

Here, *X* is a document-term matrix that can be generated using the **tm** package and *K* is the number of topics. The method is the method to be used for fitting. There are two methods that are supported: Gibbs and VEM.

Let's do a small example of building LDA models using this package. The dataset used is the **Reuter_50_50** dataset from the UCI Machine Learning repository (references 10 and 11 in the *References* section of this chapter). The dataset can be downloaded from https://archive.ics.uci.edu/ml/datasets/Reuter_50_50. For this exercise, we will only use documents from one directory, namely AlanCrosby in the C50train directory. The required preprocessing can be done using the following R script; readers should have installed the tm and topicmodels packages before trying this exercise:

```
>library(topicmodels)
>library(tm)
>#creation of training corpus from reuters dataset
>dirsourcetrain <- DirSource(directory
          = "C:/…/C50/C50train/AaronPressman")
>xtrain <- VCorpus(dirsourcetrain)
>#remove extra white space
>xtrain <- tm_map(xtrain,stripWhitespace)
>#changing to lower case
>xtrain <- tm_map(xtrain,content_transformer(tolower))
>#removing stop words
>xtrain <- tm_map(xtrain,removeWords,stopwords("english"))
>#stemming the document
>xtrain <- tm_map(xtrain,stemDocument)
>#creating Document-Term Matrix
>xtrain <-  as.data.frame.matrix(DocumentTermMatrix(xtrain))
```

The same set of steps can be used to create the test dataset from the /…/C50/C50test/ directory.

Once we have the document-term matrices `xtrain` and `xtest`, the LDA model can be built and tested using the following R script:

```
>#training lda model
>ldamodel <- LDA(xtrain,10,method = "VEM")
>#computation of perplexity, on training data (only with VEM method)
>perp <- perplexity(ldamodel)
>perp
[1] 407.3006
```

A value of perplexity around 100 indicates a good fit. In this case, we need to add more training data or change the value of *K* to improve perplexity.

Now let's use the trained LDA model to predict the topics on the test dataset:

```
>#extracting topics from test data)
>postprob <- posterior(ldamodel,xtest)
>postprob$topics
                     1          2          3          4         5         6         7          8          9         10
42764newsML.txt 0.03342815 0.101639 0.01807829 0.01622083 0.1978855 0.2641093 0.2065814 0.05056069 0.07114902 0.04034784
```

Here, the test set contains only one file, namely `42764newsML.txt`. The distribution of its topic among the 10 topics produced by the LDA model is shown.

The lda package

The lda package was developed by Jonathan Chang and he implemented a collapsed Gibbs sampling method for the estimation of posterior. The package can be downloaded from the CRAN website at `http://cran.r-project.org/web/packages/lda/index.html`.

The main function in the package, `lda.collapsed.gibbs.sampler`, uses a collapsed Gibbs sampler to fit three different models. These are **Latent Dirichlet allocation (LDA)**, **supervised LDA (sLDA)**, and the **mixed membership stochastic blockmodel (MMSB)**. These functions take input documents and return point estimates of latent parameters. These functions can be used in R as follows:

```
>lda.collapsed.gibbs.sampler(documents,K,vocab,num.iterations,
  alpha,eta,initial
= NULL,burnin = NULL,compute.log.likelihood = FALSE,trace
= 0L,freeze.topics = FALSE)
```

Here, `documents` represents a list containing documents, the length of the list is equal to `D`, and `K` is the number of topics; `vocab` is a character vector specifying the vocabulary of words; `alpha` and `eta` are the values of hyperparameters.

Exercises

1. For the Reuter_50_50 dataset, fit the LDA model using the `lda.collapsed.gibbs.sampler` function in the lda package and compare performance with that of the topicmodels package. Note that you need to convert the document-term matrix to lda format using the `dtm2ldaformat( )` function in the topicmodels package in order to use the lda package.

References

1. Bouwmans, T., El Baf F., and "Vachon B. Background Modeling Using Mixture of Gaussians for Foreground Detection – A Survey" (PDF). Recent Patents on Computer Science 1: 219-237. 2008

2. Bishop C.M. *Pattern Recognition and Machine Learning*. Springer. 2006

3. Biecek P., Szczurek E., Tiuryn J., and Vingron M. "The R Package bgmm: Mixture Modeling with Uncertain Knowledge". Journal of Statistical Software. Volume 47, Issue 3. 2012

4. Bruno B., Mastrogiovanni F., Sgorbissa A., Vernazza T., and Zaccaria R. "Analysis of human behavior recognition algorithms based on acceleration data". In: IEEE Int Conf on Robotics and Automation (ICRA), pp. 1602-1607. 2013

5. Bruno B., Mastrogiovanni F., Sgorbissa A., Vernazza T., and Zaccaria R. "Human Motion Modeling and Recognition: A computational approach". In: IEEE International Conference on Automation Science and Engineering (CASE). pp 156-161. 2012

6. Hofmann T. "Probabilistic Latent Semantic Indexing". In: Twenty-Second Annual International SIGIR Conference. 1999

7. Blei D.M., Jordan M.I., and Ng A.Y. "Latent Dirichlet Allocation". Journal of Machine Learning Research 3. 993-1022. 2003

8. Blei D.M., and Lafferty J.D. "A Correlated Topic Model of Science". The Annals of Applied Statistics. 1(1), 17-35. 2007

9. Phan X.H., Nguyen L.M., and Horguchi S. "Learning to Classify Short and Sparse Text & Web with Hidden Topics from Large-scale Data Collections". In: 17th International World Wide Web Conference (WWW 2008). pages 91-100. Beijing, China. 2008

Summary

In this chapter, we discussed the concepts behind unsupervised and semi-supervised machine learning, and their Bayesian treatment. We learned two important Bayesian unsupervised models: the Bayesian mixture model and LDA. We discussed in detail the bgmm package for the Bayesian mixture model, and the topicmodels and lda packages for topic modeling. Since the subject of unsupervised learning is vast, we could only cover a few Bayesian methods in this chapter, just to give a flavor of the subject. We have not covered semi-supervised methods using both item labeling and feature labeling. Interested readers should refer to more specialized books in this subject. In the next chapter, we will learn another important class of models, namely neural networks.

8
Bayesian Neural Networks

As the name suggests, artificial neural networks are statistical models built taking inspirations from the architecture and cognitive capabilities of biological brains. Neural network models typically have a layered architecture consisting of a large number of neurons in each layer, and neurons between different layers are connected. The first layer is called input layer, the last layer is called output layer, and the rest of the layers in the middle are called hidden layers. Each neuron has a state that is determined by a nonlinear function of the state of all neurons connected to it. Each connection has a weight that is determined from the training data containing a set of input and output pairs. This kind of layered architecture of neurons and their connections is present in the **neocortex** region of human brain and is considered to be responsible for higher functions such as sensory perception and language understanding.

The first computational model for neural network was proposed by Warren McCulloch and Walter Pitts in 1943. Around the same time, psychologist Donald Hebb created a hypothesis of learning based on the mechanism of excitation and adaptation of neurons that is known as **Hebb's rule**. The hypothesis can be summarized by saying *Neurons that fire together, wire together*. Although there were several researchers who tried to implement computational models of neural networks, it was Frank Rosenblatt in 1958 who first created an algorithm for pattern recognition using a two-layer neural network called **Perceptron**.

The research and applications of neural networks had both stagnant and great periods of progress during 1970-2010. Some of the landmarks in the history of neural networks are the invention of the **backpropagation** algorithm by Paul Werbos in 1975, a fast learning algorithm for learning multilayer neural networks (also called **deep learning networks**) by Geoffrey Hinton in 2006, and the use of GPGPUs to achieve greater computational power required for processing neural networks in the latter half of the last decade.

Today, neural network models and their applications have again taken a central stage in artificial intelligence with applications in computer vision, speech recognition, and natural language understanding. This is the reason this book has devoted one chapter specifically to this subject. The importance of Bayesian inference in neural network models will become clear when we go into detail in later sections.

Two-layer neural networks

Let us look at the formal definition of a two-layer neural network. We follow the notations and description used by David MacKay (reference 1, 2, and 3 in the *References* section of this chapter). The input to the NN is given by $X = \{X_1, X_2, \cdots, X_N\}$. The input values are first multiplied by a set of weights to produce a weighted linear combination and then transformed using a nonlinear function to produce values of the state of neurons in the hidden layer:

$$a_j^{(1)} = \sum_l w_{jl}^{(1)} X_l + \theta_j^{(1)}; \quad h_j = f^{(1)}\left(a_j^{(1)}\right)$$

A similar operation is done at the second layer to produce final output values Y_i:

$$a_j^{(2)} = \sum_j w_{ij}^{(2)} h_j + \theta_i^{(2)}; \quad Y_i = f^{(2)}\left(a_j^{(2)}\right)$$

The function $f(\ )$ is usually taken as either a **sigmoid** function $f(x) = 1/(1 + exp(-x))$ or $f(x) = \tanh(x)$. Another common function used for multiclass classification is **softmax** defined as follows:

$$f(x)_i = \frac{exp(x_i)}{\sum_{k=1}^{K} exp(x_k)}$$

This is a normalized exponential function.

All these are highly nonlinear functions exhibiting the property that the output value has a sharp increase as a function of the input. This nonlinear property gives neural networks more computational flexibility than standard linear or generalized linear models. Here, θ is called a bias parameter. The weights $\{w_{ij}\}$ together with biases $\{\theta_i\}$ form the weight vector $\mathbf{w}$.

The schematic structure of the two-layer neural network is shown here:

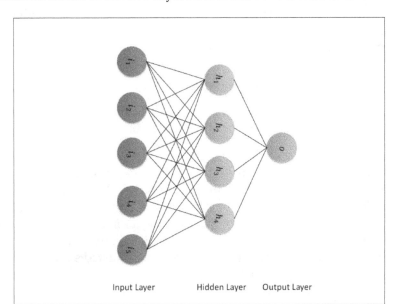

The learning in neural networks corresponds to finding the value of weight vector such as **w**, such that for a given dataset consisting of ground truth values input and target (output), $D = \{X^{(m)}, T^{(m)}\}$, the error of prediction of target values by the network is minimum. For regression problems, this is achieved by minimizing the error function:

$$E_D(\mathbf{w}) = \frac{1}{2} \sum_{m=1}^{M} \left(T^{(m)} - Y\left(X^{(m)}; \mathbf{w}\right) \right)^2$$

For the classification task, in neural network training, instead of squared error one uses a cross entropy defined as follows:

$$E_D(\mathbf{w}) = \frac{1}{M} \sum_{m=1}^{M} \log Y\left(X^{(m)}; \mathbf{w}\right)$$

To avoid overfitting, a regularization term is usually also included in the objective function. The form of the regularization function is usually $E_W = \frac{1}{2}\Sigma_i w_i^2$, which gives penalty to large values of **w**, reducing the chances of overfitting. The resulting objective function is as follows:

$$M(w) = \beta E_D + \alpha E_W$$

Here, α and β are free parameters for which the optimum values can be found from cross-validation experiments.

To minimize $M(\mathbf{w})$ with respect to **w**, one uses the backpropagation algorithm as described in the classic paper by Rumelhart, Hinton, and Williams (reference 3 in the *References* section of this chapter). In the backpropagation for each input/output pair, the value of the predicted output is computed using a forward pass from the input layer. The error, or the difference between the predicted output and actual output, is propagated back and at each node, the weights are readjusted so that the error is a minimum.

Bayesian treatment of neural networks

To set the neural network learning in a Bayesian context, consider the error function E_D for the regression case. It can be treated as a Gaussian noise term for observing the given dataset conditioned on the weights **w**. This is precisely the likelihood function that can be written as follows:

$$P(D \mid w, \beta, \mathcal{H}) = \frac{1}{Z_D(\beta)} exp(-\beta E_D)$$

Here, β is the variance of the noise term given by $\sigma_v^2 = 1/\beta$ and $\mathcal{H}$ represents a probabilistic model. The regularization term can be considered as the log of the prior probability distribution over the parameters:

$$P(w \mid \alpha, H) = \frac{1}{Z_w(\alpha)} exp(-\alpha E_w)$$

Here, $\sigma_w^2 = 1/\alpha$ is the variance of the prior distribution of weights. It can be easily shown using Bayes' theorem that the objective function $M(\mathbf{w})$ then corresponds to the posterior distribution of parameters $\mathbf{w}$:

$$P(\mathbf{w}\,|\,D,\alpha,\beta,\mathcal{H}) = \frac{P(D\,|\,\mathbf{w},\beta,\mathcal{H})\,P(\mathbf{w}\,|\,\alpha,\mathcal{H})}{P(D\,|\,\alpha,\beta,\mathcal{H})}$$

In the neural network case, we are interested in the local maxima of $P(\mathbf{w}\,|\,D,\alpha,\beta,\mathcal{H})$. The posterior is then approximated as a Gaussian around each maxima w_{MP}, as follows:

$$P(\mathbf{w}\,|\,D,\alpha,\beta,\mathcal{H}) \approx \frac{1}{Z_M'} exp\left(-M(\mathbf{w}_{MP}) - \frac{1}{2}(\mathbf{w} - \mathbf{w}_{MP})^T A(\mathbf{w} - \mathbf{w}_{MP}) \right)$$

Here, A is a matrix of the second derivative of $M(\mathbf{w})$ with respect to $\mathbf{w}$ and represents an inverse of the covariance matrix. It is also known by the name **Hessian** matrix.

The value of hyper parameters α and β is found using the **evidence framework**. In this, the probability $P(D\,|\,\alpha,\beta,\mathcal{H})$ is used as a evidence to find the best values of α and β from data D. This is done through the following Bayesian rule:

$$P(\alpha,\beta\,|\,D,\mathcal{H}) = \frac{P(D\,|\,\alpha,\beta,\mathcal{H})\,P(\alpha,\beta\,|\,H)}{P(D\,|\,\mathcal{H})}$$

By using the evidence framework and Gaussian approximation of posterior (references 2 and 5 in the *References* section of this chapter), one can show that the best value of $\alpha = \alpha_{MP}$ satisfies the following:

$$\frac{1}{\alpha_{MP}} = \frac{1}{\gamma}\sum_i \left[w_i^{MP^2} \right]$$

Also, the best value of $\beta = \beta_{MP}$ satisfies the following:

$$\frac{1}{\beta_{MP}} = \frac{2E_D}{N - \gamma}$$

In these equations, γ is the number of well-determined parameters given by $\gamma = k - \alpha\,Trace\left(A^{-1}\right)$ where k is the length of **w**.

The brnn R package

The **brnn** package was developed by Paulino Perez Rodriguez and Daniel Gianola, and it implements the two-layer Bayesian regularized neural network described in the previous section. The main function in the package is `brnn( )` that can be called using the following command:

```
>brnn(x,y,neurons,normalize,epochs,…,Monte_Carlo,…)
```

Here, x is an $n \times p$ matrix where n is the number of data points and p is the number of variables; y is an n dimensional vector containing target values. The number of neurons in the hidden layer of the network can be specified by the variable `neurons`. If the indicator function `normalize` is TRUE, it will normalize the input and output, which is the default option. The maximum number of iterations during model training is specified using `epochs`. If the indicator binary variable `Monte_Carlo` is true, then an MCMC method is used to estimate the trace of the inverse of the Hessian matrix A.

Let us try an example with the Auto MPG dataset that we used in *Chapter 5, Bayesian Regression Models*. The following R code will import data, create training and test sets, train a neural network model using training data, and make predictions for the test set:

```
>install.packages("brnn")  #one time installation
>library(brnn)
>mpgdataall <- read.csv("C:/…/auto-mpg.csv")#give the correct full
path
>mpgdata <- mpgdataall[,c(1,3,5,6)]
>#Fitting Bayesian NN Model
>ytrain <- mpgdata[1:100,1]
>xtrain <- as.matrix(mpgdata[1:100,2:4])
>mpg_brnn <- brnn(xtrain,ytrain,neurons=2,normalize = TRUE,epochs
        = 1000,Monte_Carlo = TRUE)
>summary(mpg_brnn)
A Bayesian regularized neural network
3 - 2 - 1 with 10 weights,biases and connection strengths
Inputs and output were normalized
Training finished because Changes in F
        = beta*SCE + alpha*Ew in last 3 iterations less than 0.001
```

```
>#Prediction using trained model
>ytest <- mpgdata[101:150,1]
>xtest <- as.matrix(mpgdata[101:150,2:4])
>ypred_brnn <- predict.brnn(mpg_brnn,xtest)
>plot(ytest,ypred_brnn)
>err <-ytest-ypred
>summary(err)
```

Deep belief networks and deep learning

Some of the pioneering advancements in neural networks research in the last decade have opened up a new frontier in machine learning that is generally called by the name **deep learning** (references 5 and 7 in the *References* section of this chapter). The general definition of deep learning is, *a class of machine learning techniques, where many layers of information processing stages in hierarchical supervised architectures are exploited for unsupervised feature learning and for pattern analysis/classification. The essence of deep learning is to compute hierarchical features or representations of the observational data, where the higher-level features or factors are defined from lower-level ones* (reference 8 in the *References* section of this chapter). Although there are many similar definitions and architectures for deep learning, two common elements in all of them are: *multiple layers of nonlinear information processing* and *supervised or unsupervised learning of feature representations at each layer from the features learned at the previous layer*. The initial works on deep learning were based on multilayer neural network models. Recently, many other forms of models have also been used, such as deep kernel machines and deep Q-networks.

Even in previous decades, researchers have experimented with multilayer neural networks. However, two reasons limited any progress with learning using such architectures. The first reason is that the learning of the network parameters is a non-convex optimization problem. Starting from random initial conditions, one gets stuck at local minima during minimization of error. The second reason is that the associated computational requirements were huge. A breakthrough for the first problem came when Geoffrey Hinton developed a fast algorithm for learning a special class of neural networks called **deep belief nets** (DBN). We will describe DBNs in more detail in later sections. The high computational power requirements were met with the advancement in computing using **general purpose graphical processing units** (GPGPUs). What made deep learning so popular for practical applications is the significant improvement in accuracy achieved in automatic speech recognition and computer vision. For example, the **word error rate** in automatic speech recognition of a switchboard conversational speech had reached a saturation of around 40% after years of research.

However, using deep learning, the word error rate reduced dramatically to close to 10% in a matter of a few years. Another well-known example is how **deep convolution neural network** achieved the least error rate of 15.3% in the 2012 ImageNet Large Scale Visual Recognition Challenge compared to state-of-the-art methods that gave 26.2% as the least error rate (reference 7 in the *References* section of this chapter).

In this chapter, we will describe one class of deep learning models called deep belief networks. Interested readers may wish to read the book by Li Deng and Dong Yu (reference 9 in the *References* section of this chapter) for a detailed understanding of various methods and applications of deep learning. We will follow their notations in the rest of the chapter. We will also illustrate the use of DBN with the R package **darch**.

Restricted Boltzmann machines

A **restricted Boltzmann machine (RBM)** is a two-layer network (bi-partite graph), in which one layer is a visible layer (*v*) and the second layer is a hidden layer (*h*). All nodes in the visible layer and all nodes in the hidden layer are connected by undirected edges, and there no connections between nodes in the same layer:

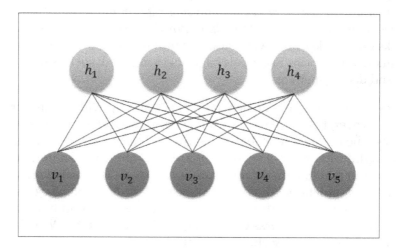

An RBM is characterized by the joint distribution of states of all visible units $v = \{v_1, v_2, \cdots, v_M\}$ and states of all hidden units $h = \{h_1, h_2, \cdots, h_N\}$ given by:

$$P(v, h \mid \theta) = \frac{\exp\left(-E\left(v, h \mid \theta\right)\right)}{Z}$$

Here, $E(v,h|\theta)$ is called the **energy function** and $Z = \sum_v \sum_h \exp(-E(v,h|\theta))$ is the normalization constant known by the name **partition function** from Statistical Physics nomenclature.

There are mainly two types of RBMs. In the first one, both v and h are Bernoulli random variables. In the second type, h is a Bernoulli random variable whereas v is a Gaussian random variable. For Bernoulli RBM, the energy function is given by:

$$E(v,h|\theta) = -\sum_{i=1}^{M}\sum_{j=1}^{N} w_{ij}v_i h_j - \sum_{i=1}^{M} b_i v_i - \sum_{j=1}^{N} a_j h_j$$

Here, w_{ij} represents the weight of the edge between nodes v_i and h_j; b_i and a_j are bias parameters for the visible and hidden layers respectively. For this energy function, the exact expressions for the conditional probability can be derived as follows:

$$p\left(h_j = 1 \mid v;\theta\right) = \sigma\left(\sum_{i=1}^{M} w_{ij} v_i + a_j\right)$$

$$p\left(v_i = 1 \mid h;\theta\right) = \sigma\left(\sum_{i=1}^{M} w_{ij} h_j + b_i\right)$$

Here, $\sigma(x)$ is the logistic function $1/(1+\exp(-x))$.

If the input variables are continuous, one can use the Gaussian RBM; the energy function of it is given by:

$$E(v,h|\theta) = -\sum_{i=1}^{M}\sum_{j=1}^{N} w_{ij}v_i h_j - \frac{1}{2}\sum_{i=1}^{M}(v_i - b_i)^2 - \sum_{j=1}^{N} a_j h_j$$

Also, in this case, the conditional probabilities of v_i and h_j will become as follows:

$$p\left(h_j = 1 \mid v;\theta\right) = \sigma\left(\sum_{i=1}^{M} w_{ij} v_i + a_j\right)$$

$$p\left(v_i, h;\theta\right) = N\left(v_i; \sum_{i=1}^{M} w_{ij} h_j + b_i, 1\right)$$

This is a normal distribution with mean $\sum_{i=1}^{M} w_{ij} h_j + b_i$ and variance 1.

Now that we have described the basic architecture of an RBM, how is it that it is trained? If we try to use the standard approach of taking the gradient of log-likelihood, we get the following update rule:

$$\Delta w_{ij} = \mathbb{E}_{data}\left(v_i h_j\right) - \mathbb{E}_{model}\left(v_i h_j\right)$$

Here, $\mathbb{E}_{data}(v_i h_j)$ is the expectation of $v_i h_j$ computed using the dataset and $\mathbb{E}_{model}(v_i h_j)$ is the same expectation computed using the model. However, one cannot use this exact expression for updating weights because $\mathbb{E}_{model}(v_i h_j)$ is difficult to compute.

The first breakthrough came to solve this problem and, hence, to train deep neural networks, when Hinton and team proposed an algorithm called **Contrastive Divergence (CD)** (reference 7 in the *References* section of this chapter). The essence of the algorithm is described in the next paragraph.

The idea is to approximate $\mathbb{E}_{model}(v_i h_j)$ by using values of v_i and h_j generated using Gibbs sampling from the conditional distributions mentioned previously. One scheme of doing this is as follows:

1. Initialize $v^{t=0}$ from the dataset.
2. Find $h^{t=0}$ by sampling from the conditional distribution $h^{t=0} \sim p\left(h \mid v^{t=0}\right)$.
3. Find $v^{t=1}$ by sampling from the conditional distribution $v^{t=1} \sim p\left(v \mid h^{t=0}\right)$.
4. Find $h^{t=1}$ by sampling from the conditional distribution $h^{t=1} \sim p\left(h \mid v^{t=1}\right)$.

Once we find the values of $v^{t=1}$ and $h^{t=1}$, use $\left(v_i^{t=1} h_j^{t=1}\right)$, which is the product of ith component of $v^{t=1}$ and j^{th} component of $h^{t=1}$, as an approximation for $\mathbb{E}_{model}(v_i h_j)$. This is called **CD-1 algorithm**. One can generalize this to use the values from the kth step of Gibbs sampling and it is known as **CD-k algorithm**. One can easily see the connection between RBMs and Bayesian inference. Since the CD algorithm is like a posterior density estimate, one could say that RBMs are trained using a Bayesian inference approach.

Although the Contrastive Divergence algorithm looks simple, one needs to be very careful in training RBMs, otherwise the model can result in overfitting. Readers who are interested in using RBMs in practical applications should refer to the technical report (reference 10 in the *References* section of this chapter), where this is discussed in detail.

Deep belief networks

One can stack several RBMs, one on top of each other, such that the values of hidden units in the layer $n-1\left(h_{i,n-1}\right)$ would become values of visible units in the nth layer $\left(v_{i,n}\right)$, and so on. The resulting network is called a deep belief network. It was one of the main architectures used in early deep learning networks for pretraining. The idea of pretraining a NN is the following: in the standard three-layer (input-hidden-output) NN, one can start with random initial values for the weights and using the backpropagation algorithm, can find a good minimum of the log-likelihood function. However, when the number of layers increases, the straightforward application of backpropagation does not work because starting from output layer, as we compute the gradient values for the layers deep inside, their magnitude becomes very small. This is called the **gradient vanishing** problem. As a result, the network will get trapped in some poor local minima. Backpropagation still works if we are starting from the neighborhood of a good minimum. To achieve this, a DNN is often pretrained in an unsupervised way, using a DBN. Instead of starting from random values of weights, train a DBN in an unsupervised way and use weights from the DBN as initial weights for a corresponding supervised DNN. It was seen that such DNNs pretrained using DBNs perform much better (reference 8 in the *References* section of this chapter).

The layer-wise pretraining of a DBN proceeds as follows. Start with the first RBM and train it using input data in the visible layer and the CD algorithm (or its latest better variants). Then, stack a second RBM on top of this. For this RBM, use values sample from $p(h|v,\theta)$ as the values for the visible layer. Continue this process for the desired number of layers. The outputs of hidden units from the top layer can also be used as inputs for training a supervised model. For this, add a conventional NN layer at the top of DBN with the desired number of classes as the number of output nodes. Input for this NN would be the output from the top layer of DBN. This is called **DBN-DNN architecture**. Here, a DBN's role is generating highly efficient features (the output of the top layer of DBN) automatically from the input data for the supervised NN in the top layer.

The architecture of a five-layer DBN-DNN for a binary classification task is shown in the following figure:

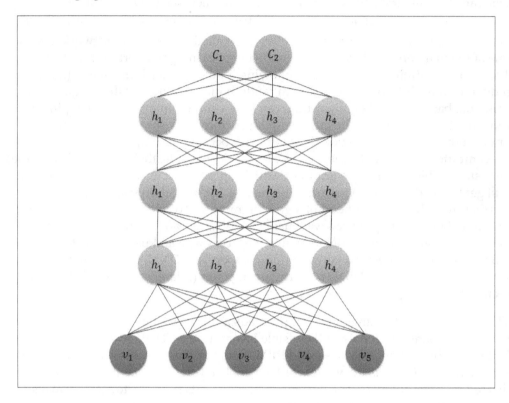

The last layer is trained using the backpropagation algorithm in a supervised manner for the two classes C_1 and C_2. We will illustrate the training and classification with such a DBN-DNN using the darch R package.

The darch R package

The darch package, written by Martin Drees, is one of the R packages using which one can begin doing deep learning in R. It implements the DBN described in the previous section (references 5 and 7 in the *References* section of this chapter). The package can be downloaded from `https://cran.r-project.org/web/packages/darch/index.html`.

The main class in the darch package implements deep architectures and provides the ability to train them with Contrastive Divergence and fine-tune with backpropagation, resilient backpropagation, and conjugate gradients. The new instances of the class are created with the newDArch constructor. It is called with the following arguments: a vector containing the number of nodes in each layers, the batch size, a Boolean variable to indicate whether to use the **ff** package for computing weights and outputs, and the name of the function for generating the weight matrices. Let us create a network having two input units, four hidden units, and one output unit:

```
install.packages("darch") #one time
>library(darch)
>darch <- newDArch(c(2,4,1),batchSize = 2,genWeightFunc
      = generateWeights)
INFO [2015-07-19 18:50:29] Constructing a darch with 3 layers.
INFO [2015-07-19 18:50:29] Generating RBMs.
INFO [2015-07-19 18:50:29] Construct new RBM instance with 2 visible
and 4 hidden units.
INFO [2015-07-19 18:50:29] Construct new RBM instance with 4 visible
and 1 hidden units.
```

Let us train the DBN with a toy dataset. We are using this because for training any realistic examples, it would take a long time: hours, if not days. Let us create an input data set containing two columns and four rows:

```
>inputs <- matrix(c(0,0,0,1,1,0,1,1),ncol=2,byrow=TRUE)
>outputs <- matrix(c(0,1,1,0),nrow=4)
```

Now, let us pretrain the DBN, using the input data:

```
>darch <- preTrainDArch(darch,inputs,maxEpoch=1000)
```

We can have a look at the weights learned at any layer using the getLayerWeights( ) function. Let us see how the hidden layer looks:

```
>getLayerWeights(darch,index=1)
[[1]]
           [,1]          [,2]        [,3]        [,4]
[1,]    8.167022     0.4874743  -7.563470  -6.951426
[2,]    2.024671   -10.7012389   1.313231   1.070006
[3,]   -5.391781     5.5878931   3.254914   3.000914
```

Now, let's do a backpropagation for supervised learning. For this, we need to first set the layer functions to `sigmoidUnitDerivatives`:

```
>layers <- getLayers(darch)
>for(i in length(layers):1){
    layers[[i]][[2]] <- sigmoidUnitDerivative
    }
>setLayers(darch) <- layers
>rm(layers)
```

Finally, the following two lines perform the backpropagation:

```
>setFineTuneFunction(darch) <- backpropagation
>darch <- fineTuneDArch(darch,inputs,outputs,maxEpoch=1000)
```

We can see the prediction quality of DBN on the training data itself by running `darch` as follows:

```
>darch <- getExecuteFunction(darch)(darch,inputs)
>outputs_darch <- getExecOutputs(darch)
>outputs_darch[[2]]
        [,1]
[1,]  9.998474e-01
[2,]  4.921130e-05
[3,]  9.997649e-01
[4,]  3.796699e-05
```

Comparing with the actual output, DBN has predicted the wrong output for the first and second input rows. Since this example was just to illustrate how to use the darch package, we are not worried about the 50% accuracy here.

Other deep learning packages in R

Although there are other deep learning packages in R, such as **deepnet** and **RcppDL**, compared with libraries in other languages such as **Cuda** (C++) and **Theano** (Python), R yet does not have good native libraries for deep learning. The only available package is a wrapper for the Java-based deep learning open source project H2O. This R package, **h2o**, allows running H2O via its REST API from within R. Readers who are interested in serious deep learning projects and applications should use H2O using h2o packages in R. One needs to install H2O in your machine to use h2o. We will cover H2O in the next chapter when we discuss Big Data and the distributed computing platform called Spark.

Exercises

1. For the Auto MPG dataset, compare the performance of predictive models using ordinary regression, Bayesian GLM, and Bayesian neural networks.

References

1. MacKay D. J. C. *Information Theory, Inference and Learning Algorithms.* Cambridge University Press. 2003. ISBN-10: 0521642981

2. MacKayD. J. C. "The Evidence Framework Applied to Classification Networks". Neural Computation. Volume 4(3), 698-714. 1992

3. MacKay D. J. C. "Probable Networks and Plausible Predictions – a review of practical Bayesian methods for supervised neural networks". Network: Computation in neural systems

4. Hinton G. E., Rumelhart D. E., and Williams R. J. "Learning Representations by Back Propagating Errors". Nature. Volume 323, 533-536. 1986

5. MacKay D. J. C. "Bayesian Interpolation". Neural Computation. Volume 4(3), 415-447. 1992

6. Hinton G. E., Krizhevsky A., and Sutskever I. "ImageNet Classification with Deep Convolutional Neural Networks". Advances In Neural Information Processing Systems (NIPS). 2012

7. Hinton G., Osindero S., and Teh Y. "A Fast Learning Algorithm for Deep Belief Nets". Neural Computation. 18:1527–1554. 2006

8. Hinton G. and Salakhutdinov R. "Reducing the Dimensionality of Data with Neural Networks". Science. 313(5786):504–507. 2006

9. Li Deng and Dong Yu. *Deep Learning: Methods and Applications (Foundations and Trends(r) in Signal Processing).* Now Publishers Inc. Vol 7, Issue 3-4. 2014. ISBN-13: 978-1601988140

10. Hinton G. "A Practical Guide to Training Restricted Boltzmann Machines". UTML Tech Report 2010-003. Univ. Toronto. 2010

Summary

In this chapter, we learned about an important class of machine learning model, namely neural networks, and their Bayesian implementation. These models are inspired by the architecture of the human brain and they continue to be an area of active research and development. We also learned one of the latest advances in neural networks that is called deep learning. It can be used to solve many problems such as computer vision and natural language processing that involves highly cognitive elements. The artificial intelligent systems using deep learning were able to achieve accuracies comparable to human intelligence in tasks such as speech recognition and image classification. With this chapter, we have covered important classes of Bayesian machine learning models. In the next chapter, we will look at a different aspect: large scale machine learning and some of its applications in Bayesian models.

Bayesian Modeling at Big Data Scale

When we learned the principles of Bayesian inference in *Chapter 3*, *Introducing Bayesian Inference*, we saw that as the amount of training data increases, contribution to the parameter estimation from data overweighs that from the prior distribution. Also, the uncertainty in parameter estimation decreases. Therefore, you may wonder why one needs Bayesian modeling in large-scale data analysis. To answer this question, let us look at one such problem, which is building recommendation systems for e-commerce products.

In a typical e-commerce store, there will be millions of users and tens of thousands of products. However, each user would have purchased only a small fraction (less than 10%) of all the products found in the store in their lifetime. Let us say the e-commerce store is collecting users' feedback for each product sold as a rating on a scale of 1 to 5. Then, the store can create a user-product rating matrix to capture the ratings of all users. In this matrix, rows would correspond to users and columns would correspond to products. The entry of each cell would be the rating given by the user (corresponding to the row) to the product (corresponding to the column). Now, it is easy to see that although the overall size of this matrix is huge, only less than 10% entries would have values since every user would have bought only less than 10% products from the store. So, this is a highly sparse dataset. Whenever there is a machine learning task where, even though the overall data size is huge, the data is highly sparse, overfitting can happen and one should rely on Bayesian methods (reference 1 in the *References* section of this chapter). Also, many models such as Bayesian networks, Latent Dirichlet allocation, and deep belief networks are built on the Bayesian inference paradigm.

When these models are trained on a large dataset, such as text corpora from Reuters, then the underlying problem is large-scale Bayesian modeling. As it is, Bayesian modeling is computationally intensive since we have to estimate the whole posterior distribution of parameters and also do model averaging of the predictions. The presence of large datasets will make the situation even worse. So what are the computing frameworks that we can use to do Bayesian learning at a large scale using R? In the next two sections, we will discuss some of the latest developments in this area.

Distributed computing using Hadoop

In the last decade, tremendous progress was made in distributed computing when two research engineers from Google developed a computing paradigm called the **MapReduce** framework and an associated distributed filesystem called Google File System (reference 2 in the *References* section of this chapter). Later on, Yahoo developed an open source version of this distributed filesystem named **Hadoop** that became the hallmark of Big Data computing. Hadoop is ideal for processing large amounts of data, which cannot fit into the memory of a single large computer, by distributing the data into multiple computers and doing the computation on each node locally from the disk. An example would be extracting relevant information from log files, where typically the size of data for a month would be in the order of terabytes.

To use Hadoop, one has to write programs using MapReduce framework to parallelize the computing. A Map operation splits the data into multiple key-value pairs and sends it to different nodes. At each of those nodes, a computation is done on each of the key-value pairs. Then, there is a shuffling operation where all the pairs with the same value of key are brought together. After this, a Reduce operation sums up all the results corresponding to the same key from the previous computation step. Typically, these MapReduce operations can be written using a high-level language called **Pig**. One can also write MapReduce programs in R using the **RHadoop** package, which we will describe in the next section.

RHadoop for using Hadoop from R

RHadoop is a collection of open source packages using which an R user can manage and analyze data stored in the **Hadoop Distributed File System** (HDFS). In the background, RHadoop will translate these as MapReduce operations in Java and run them on HDFS.

The various packages in RHadoop and their uses are as follows:

- **rhdfs**: Using this package, a user can connect to an HDFS from R and perform basic actions such as read, write, and modify files.

- **rhbase**: This is the package to connect to a HBASE database from R and to read, write, and modify tables.

- **plyrmr**: Using this package, an R user can do the common data manipulation tasks such as the slicing and dicing of datasets. This is similar to the function of packages such as **plyr** or **reshape2**.

- **rmr2**: Using this package, a user can write MapReduce functions in R and execute them in an HDFS.

Unlike the other packages discussed in this book, the packages associated with RHadoop are not available from CRAN. They can be downloaded from the GitHub repository at `https://github.com/RevolutionAnalytics` and are installed from the local drive.

Here is a sample MapReduce code written using the rmr2 package to count the number of words in a corpus (reference 3 in the *References* section of this chapter):

1. The first step involves loading the `rmr2` library:

```
>library(rmr2)
>LOCAL <- T #to execute rmr2 locally
```

2. The second step involves writing the Map function. This function takes each line in the text document and splits it into words. Each word is taken as a token. The function emits key-value pairs where each distinct word is a *key* and *value = 1*:

```
>#map function
>map.wc <- function(k,lines){
       words.list <- strsplit(lines,'\\s+^' )
        words <- unlist(words.list)
        return(keyval(words,1))
     }
```

3. The third step involves writing a reduce function. This function groups all the same *key* from different mappers and sums their *value*. Since, in this case, each word is a *key* and the *value = 1*, the output of the reduce will be the count of the words:

```
>#reduce function
>reduce.wc<-function(word,counts){
         return(keyval(word,sum(counts) ))
     }
```

4. The fourth step involves writing a word count function combining the map and reduce functions and executing this function on a file named `hdfs.data` stored in the HDFS containing the input text:

```
>#word count function
>wordcount<-function(input,output=NULL){
           mapreduce(input = input,output = output,input.format =
"text",map = map.wc,reduce = reduce.wc,combine = T)
}
>out<-wordcount(hdfs.data,hdfs.out)
```

5. The fifth step involves getting the output file from HDFS and printing the top five lines:

```
>results<-from.dfs(out)
>results.df<-as.data.frame(results,stringAsFactors=F)
>colnames(results.df)<-c('word^' ,^' count^')
>head(results.df)
```

Spark – in-memory distributed computing

One of the issues with Hadoop is that after a MapReduce operation, the resulting files are written to the hard disk. Therefore, when there is a large data processing operation, there would be many read and write operations on the hard disk, which makes processing in Hadoop very slow. Moreover, the network latency, which is the time required to shuffle data between different nodes, also contributes to this problem. Another disadvantage is that one cannot make real-time queries from the files stored in HDFS. For machine learning problems, during training phase, the MapReduce will not persist over iterations. All this makes Hadoop not an ideal platform for machine learning.

A solution to this problem was invented at Berkeley University's AMP Lab in 2009. This came out of the PhD work of Matei Zaharia, a Romanian born computer scientist. His paper *Resilient Distributed Datasets: A Fault-Tolerant Abstraction for In-Memory Cluster Computing* (reference 4 in the *References* section of this chapter) gave rise to the Spark project that eventually became a fully open source project under Apache. Spark is an in-memory distributed computing framework that solves many of the problems of Hadoop mentioned earlier. Moreover, it supports more type of operations that just MapReduce. Spark can be used for processing iterative algorithms, interactive data mining, and streaming applications. It is based on an abstraction called **Resilient Distributed Datasets** (**RDD**). Similar to HDFS, it is also fault-tolerant.

Spark is written in a language called Scala. It has interfaces to use from Java and Python and from the recent version 1.4.0; it also supports R. This is called SparkR, which we will describe in the next section. The four classes of libraries available in Spark are SQL and DataFrames, Spark Streaming, MLib (machine learning), and GraphX (graph algorithms). Currently, SparkR supports only SQL and DataFrames; others are definitely in the roadmap. Spark can be downloaded from the Apache project page at http://spark.apache.org/downloads.html. Starting from 1.4.0 version, SparkR is included in Spark and no separate download is required.

SparkR

Similar to RHadoop, SparkR is an R package that allows R users to use Spark APIs through the RDD class. For example, using SparkR, users can run jobs on Spark from RStudio. SparkR can be evoked from RStudio. To enable this, include the following lines in your .Rprofile file that R uses at startup to initialize the environments:

```
Sys.setenv(SPARK_HOME/.../spark-1.5.0-bin-hadoop2.6")

#provide the correct path where spark downloaded folder is kept for
SPARK_HOME
.libPaths(c(file.path(Sys.getenv("SPARK_HOME"),""R",""lib"),".
libPaths()))
```

Once this is done, start RStudio and enter the following commands to start using SparkR:

```
>library(SparkR)
>sc <- sparkR.init(master="local")
```

As mentioned, as of the latest version 1.5 when this chapter is in writing, SparkR supports limited functionalities of R. This mainly includes data slicing and dicing and summary stat functions. The current version does not support the use of contributed R packages; however, it is planned for a future release. On machine learning, currently SparkR supports the glm( ) function. We will do an example in the next section.

Linear regression using SparkR

In the following example, we will illustrate how to use SparkR for machine learning. For this, we will use the same dataset of energy efficiency measurements that we used for linear regression in *Chapter 5, Bayesian Regression Models*:

```
>library(SparkR)
>sc <- sparkR.init(master="local")
```

```
>sqlContext <- sparkRSQL.init(sc)

#Importing data
>df <- read.csv("/Users/harikoduvely/Projects/Book/Data
    /ENB2012_data.csv",header = T)
>#Excluding variable Y2,X6,X8 and removing records from 768 containing
mainly null values
>df <- df[1:768,c(1,2,3,4,5,7,9)]
>#Converting to a Spark R Dataframe
>dfsr <- createDataFrame(sqlContext,df)
>model <- glm(Y1 ~ X1 + X2 + X3 + X4 + X5 + X7,data = dfsr,family
    = "gaussian")
 > summary(model)
```

Computing clusters on the cloud

In order to process large datasets using Hadoop and associated R packages, one needs a cluster of computers. In today's world, it is easy to get using cloud computing services provided by Amazon, Microsoft, and others. One needs to pay only for the amount of CPU and storage used. No need for upfront investments on infrastructure. The top four cloud computing services are AWS by Amazon, Azure by Microsoft, Compute Cloud by Google, and Bluemix by IBM. In this section, we will discuss running R programs on AWS. In particular, you will learn how to create an AWS instance; install R, RStudio, and other packages in that instance; develop and run machine learning models.

Amazon Web Services

Popularly known as AWS, Amazon Web Services started as an internal project in Amazon in 2002 to meet the dynamic computing requirements to support their e-commerce business. This grew as an **infrastructure as a service** and in 2006 Amazon launched two services to the world, **Simple Storage Service (S3)** and **Elastic Computing Cloud (EC2)**. From there, AWS grew at incredible pace. Today, they have more than 40 different types of services using millions of servers.

Creating and running computing instances on AWS

The best place to learn how to set up an AWS account and start using EC2 is the freely available e-book from Amazon Kindle store named *Amazon Elastic Compute Cloud (EC2) User Guide* (reference 6 in the *References* section of this chapter).

Here, we only summarize the essential steps involved in the process:

1. Create an AWS account.
2. Sign in to the AWS management console (`https://aws.amazon.com/console/`).
3. Click on the EC2 service.
4. Choose **Amazon Machine Instance (AMI)**.
5. Choose an instance type.
6. Create a public-private key-pair.
7. Configure instance.
8. Add storage.
9. Tag instance.
10. Configure a security group (policy specifying who can access the instance).
11. Review and launch the instance.

Log in to your instance using SSH (from Linux/Ubuntu), Putty (from Windows), or a browser using the private key provided at the time of configuring security and the IP address given at the time of launching. Here, we are assuming that the instance you have launched is a Linux instance.

Installing R and RStudio

To install R and RStudio, you need to be an authenticated user. So, create a new user and give the user administrative privilege (sudo). After that, execute the following steps from the Ubuntu shell:

1. Edit the `/etc/apt/sources.list` file.
2. Add the following line at the end:

   ```
   deb http://cran.rstudio.com/bin/linux/ubuntu trusty .
   ```

3. Get the keys for the repository to run:

   ```
   sudo apt-key adv  --keyserver keyserver.ubuntu.com -recv-keys
   51716619E084DAB9
   ```

4. Update the package list:

   ```
   sudo apt-get update
   ```

5. Install the latest version of R:

   ```
   sudo apt-get install r-base-core
   ```

6. Install gdebi to install Debian packages from the local disk:

```
sudo apt-get install gdebi-core
```

7. Download the RStudio package:

```
wget http://download2.rstudio.org/r-studio-server-0.99.446-amd64.
deb
```

8. Install RStudio:

```
sudo gdebi r-studio-server-0.99.446-amd64.deb
```

Once the installation is completed successfully, RStudio running on your AWS instance can be accessed from a browser. For this, open a browser and enter the URL `<your.aws.ip.no>:8787`.

If you are able to use your RStudio running on the AWS instance, you can then install other packages such as rhdfs, rmr2, and more from RStudio, build any machine learning models in R, and run them on the AWS cloud.

Apart from R and RStudio, AWS also supports Spark (and hence SparkR). In the following section, you will learn how to run Spark on an EC2 cluster.

Running Spark on EC2

You can launch and manage Spark clusters on Amazon EC2 using the `spark-ec2` script located in the `ec2` directory of Spark in your local machine. To launch a Spark cluster on EC2, use the following steps:

1. Go to the `ec2` directory in the Spark folder in your local machine.

2. Run the following command:

```
./spark-ec2 -k <keypair> -i <key-file> -s <num-slaves> launch
<cluster-name>
```

Here, `<keypair>` is the name of the keypair you used for launching the EC2 service mentioned in the *Creating and running computing instances on AWS* section of this chapter. The `<key-file>` is the path in your local machine where the private key has been downloaded and kept. The number of worker nodes is specified by `<num-slaves>`.

3. To run your programs in the cluster, first SSH into the cluster using the following command:

```
./spark-ec2 -k <keypair> -i <key-file> login <cluster-name>
```

After logging into the cluster, you can use Spark as you use on the local machine.

More details on how to use Spark on EC2 can be found in the Spark documentation and AWS documentation (references 5, 6, and 7 in the *References* section of the chapter).

Microsoft Azure

Microsoft Azure has full support for R and Spark. Microsoft had bought Revolution Analytics, a company that started building and supporting an enterprise version of R. Apart from this, Azure has a machine learning service where there are APIs for some Bayesian machine learning models as well. A nice video tutorial of how to launch instances on Azure and how to use their machine learning as a service can be found at the Microsoft Virtual Academy website (reference 8 in the *References* section of the chapter).

IBM Bluemix

Bluemix has full support for R through the full set of R libraries available on their instances. IBM also has integration of Spark into their cloud services in their roadmap plans. More details can be found at their documentation page (reference 9 in the *References* section of the chapter).

Other R packages for large scale machine learning

Apart from RHadoop and SparkR, there are several other native R packages specifically built for large-scale machine learning. Here, we give a brief overview of them. Interested readers should refer to *CRAN Task View: High-Performance and Parallel Computing with R* (reference 10 in the *References* section of the chapter).

Though R is single-threaded, there exists several packages for parallel computation in R. Some of the well-known packages are **Rmpi** (R version of the popular message passing interface), **multicore**, **snow** (for building R clusters), and **foreach**. From R 2.14.0, a new package called **parallel** started shipping with the base R. We will discuss some of its features here.

The parallel R package

The **parallel** package is built on top of the multicore and snow packages. It is useful for running a single program on multiple datasets such as K-fold cross validation. It can be used for parallelizing in a single machine over multiple CPUs/cores or across several machines. For parallelizing across a cluster of machines, it evokes MPI (message passing interface) using the Rmpi package.

We will illustrate the use of parallel package with the simple example of computing a square of numbers in the list 1:100000. This example will not work in Windows since the corresponding R does not support the multicore package. It can be tested on any Linux or OS X platform.

The sequential way of performing this operation is to use the `lapply` function as follows:

```
>nsquare <- function(n){return(n*n)}
>range <- c(1:100000)
>system.time(lapply(range,nsquare))
```

Using the `mclapply` function of the parallel package, this computation can be achieved in much less time:

```
>library(parallel) #included in R core packages, no separate
installation required
>numCores<-detectCores( )  #to find the number of cores in the machine
>system.time(mclapply(range,nsquare,mc.cores=numCores))
```

If the dataset is so large that it needs a cluster of computers, we can use the `parLapply` function to run the program over a cluster. This needs the Rmpi package:

```
>install.packages(Rmpi)#one time
>library(Rmpi)
>numNodes<-4 #number of workers nodes
>cl<-makeCluster(numNodes,type="MPI")
>system.time(parLapply(cl,range,nsquare))
>stopCluster(cl)
>mpi.exit( )
```

The foreach R package

This is a new looping construct in R that can be executed in parallel across multicores or clusters. It has two important operators: `%do%` for repeatedly doing a task and `%dopar%` for executing tasks in parallel.

For example, the squaring function we discussed in the previous section can be implemented using a single line command using the foreach package:

```
>install.packages(foreach)#one time
>install.packages(doParallel)#one time
>library(foreach)
>library(doParallel)
>system.time(foreach(i=1:100000)    %do%  i^2) #for executing
sequentially
>system.time(foreach(i=1:100000)    %dopar%  i^2) #for executing in
parallel
```

We will also do an example of quick sort using the `foreach` function:

```
>qsort<- function(x) {
  n <- length(x)
  if (n == 0) {
    x
  } else {
    p <- sample(n,1)
    smaller <- foreach(y=x[-p],.combine=c) %:% when(y <= x[p]) %do% y
    larger  <- foreach(y=x[-p],.combine=c) %:% when(y >  x[p]) %do% y
    c(qsort(smaller),x[p],qsort(larger))
  }
}
qsort(runif(12))
```

These packages are still undergoing a lot of development. They have not yet been used in a large way for Bayesian modeling. It is easy to use them for Bayesian inference applications such as Monte Carlo simulations.

Exercises

1. Revisit the classification problem in *Chapter 6, Bayesian Classification Models*. Repeat the same problem using the `glm()` function of SparkR.

2. Revisit the linear regression problem, we did in this chapter, using SparkR. After creating the AWS instance, repeat this problem using RStudio server on AWS.

References

1. "MapReduce Implementation of Variational Bayesian Probabilistic Matrix Factorization Algorithm". In: IEEE Conference on Big Data. pp 145-152. 2013

2. Dean J. and Ghemawat S. "MapReduce: Simplified Data Processing on Large Clusters". Communications of the ACM 51 (1). 107-113

3. https://github.com/jeffreybreen/tutorial-rmr2-airline/blob/master/R/1-wordcount.R

4. Chowdhury M., Das T., Dave A., Franklin M.J., Ma J., McCauley M., Shenker S., Stoica I., and Zaharia M. "Resilient Distributed Datasets: A Fault-Tolerant Abstraction for In-Memory Cluster Computing". NSDI 2012. 2012

5. *Amazon Elastic Compute Cloud (EC2) User Guide*, Kindle e-book by Amazon Web Services, updated April 9, 2014

6. Spark documentation for AWS at http://spark.apache.org/docs/latest/ec2-scripts.html

7. AWS documentation for Spark at http://aws.amazon.com/elasticmapreduce/details/spark/

8. Microsoft Virtual Academy website at http://www.microsoftvirtualacademy.com/training-courses/getting-started-with-microsoft-azure-machine-learning

9. IBM Bluemix Tutorial at http://www.ibm.com/developerworks/cloud/bluemix/quick-start-bluemix.html

10. CRAN Task View for contributed packages in R at https://cran.r-project.org/web/views/HighPerformanceComputing.html

Summary

In this last chapter of the book, we covered various frameworks to implement large-scale machine learning. These are very useful for Bayesian learning too. For example, to simulate from a posterior distribution, one could run a Gibbs sampling over a cluster of machines. We learned how to connect to Hadoop from R using the RHadoop package and how to use R with Spark using SparkR. We also discussed how to set up clusters in cloud services such as AWS and how to run Spark on them. Some of the native parallelization frameworks such as parallel and foreach functions were also covered.

The overall aim of this book was to introduce readers to the area of Bayesian modeling using R. Readers should have gained a good grasp of theory and concepts behind Bayesian machine learning models. Since the examples were mainly given for the purposes of illustration, I urge readers to apply these techniques to real-world problems to appreciate the subject of Bayesian inference more deeply.

Index

A

Akaike information criterion (AIC) **50**
allele frequencies **11**
arm package **74**
association rule mining **71**
Automatic Relevance Determination
        (ARD) **83**

B

backpropagation algorithm **113**
Bayesian averaging **68-70**
Bayesian classification models
    about **83**
    exercises **96**
    references **96**
Bayesian inference
    about **37**
    Bayesian view of uncertainty **37-41**
    exercises **59**
    for machine learning **63-65**
    references **60**
Bayesian information criterion (BIC) **50**
Bayesian logistic regression model
    about **91, 92**
    BayesLogit R package **93**
    dataset **93**
    datasets testing, preparing for **94**
    training, preparing for **94**
    using **95, 96**
Bayesian mixture models
    about **100-102**
    bgmm package **103-105**

Bayesian modeling, at Big Data scale
    exercises **139**
    references **140**
Bayesian models, for unsupervised learning
    about **99**
    exercises **110**
    references **110**
Bayesian neural networks
    exercises **127**
    references **127**
Bayesian Output Analysis Program
        (BOA) **57**
Bayesian regression models
    exercises **81**
    references **81**
Bayesian theorem **7**
Bayesian treatment, of neural
        networks **116-118**
Bayesian view of uncertainty
    about **37-41**
    future observations, predicting **59**
    posterior distribution, estimation **48**
    prior distribution, selecting **42**
BayesLogit R package **93**
Beta distribution **10**
bgmm package
    about **102**
    fully supervised GMM **103**
    partially supervised GMM **103**
    semi-supervised GMM **103**
    unsupervised GMM **103**
bias-variance tradeoff **65**
binary classification **62**
binomial distribution **9, 10**

binomlogit package 57
Bmk package 57
BoomSpikeSlab package 57
brnn R package 118

C

CD-1 algorithm 122
CD-k algorithm 122
central limit theorem 4
Classical Definition 1, 2
classification 71
clustering 71
clusters, computing on cloud
  about 134
  Amazon Web Services 134
  computing instances, creating 134
  computing instances, running on
    AWS 134-135
  IBM Bluemix 137
  Microsoft Azure 137
  R, installing 135, 136
  RStudio, installing 135, 136
  Spark, running on EC2 136, 137
common machine learning tasks
  association rules 71
  classification 71
  clustering 71
  density estimation 72
  dimensional reduction 72
  forecasting 71
  overview 70-72
  regression 71
Comprehensive R Archive Network
  (CRAN) 18
conditional probability 6, 7
conjugate distributions 46
conjugate prior for the likelihood
  function 46
Contrastive Divergence (CD) 122
Correlated Topic Models (CTM) 108
covariance 9
Cuda (C++) 126
curse of dimensionality 72

D

darch R package 124
data, managing in R
  about 19
  data, importing into R 22
  datasets, dicing 23
  datasets, slicing 23
  data structures 20, 21
  data types 19
  vectorized operations 24
data structures, R
  heterogeneous 20
  homogeneous 20
data types, R
  character 19
  complex 19
  integer 19
  logical 19
  numeric 19
data visualization
  about 30
  high-level plotting functions 31
  interactive graphics functions 33
  low-level plotting commands 32
DBN-DNN architecture 123
deep belief nets (DBN) 119
deep belief networks
  about 119, 123, 124
  darch R package 124-126
  deep learning packages 126
  restricted Boltzmann machine
    (RBM) 120-122
deep learning 119
deep learning networks 113
deepnet package 126
degree of belief 2
density estimation 72
dimensional reduction 72
Dirichlet distribution 12
distributed computing
  with Hadoop 130
divergence 58

E

econometrics 11
Elastic Computing Cloud (EC2) 134
empirical risk minimization 62
Energy efficiency dataset 74
energy function 121
Evolutionary Monte Carlo (EMC)
        algorithm package 55
exercises 13, 14
expectation-maximization (EM)
        algorithm 101
expectations 9

F

false negative or type II error 84
false positive or type I error 84
foreach R package 138
forecasting 71
frequentist approach to probability 2

G

Gamma distribution 11
Gaussian mixture model (GMM) 100
generalized linear model (GLM)
        packages 73
generalized linear regression 73, 74
general purpose graphical processing
        units (GPGPUs) 119
ggmcmc package 57
ggplot2 31
ggplot2 package 78
GibbsACOV package 57
gibbs.met package
  R packages 56
Gibbs sampling
  about 55, 56
  R packages 56, 57
gradient vanishing problem 123
grid 31

H

Hadoop 130
Hadoop Distributed File System
        (HDFS) 130
Hebb's rule 113
high-level plotting functions 31
Hinge loss function 62

I

IBM Bluemix 137
integrated Development environment
        (IDE) 18
interactive graphics functions 33

K

kernel density estimation (KDE) 72

L

Laplace approximation 49, 50
Latent Dirichlet allocation (LDA) 71
  about 106-109
  R packages 107
lattice 31
lda package 57, 109, 110
linear regression
  using SparkR 133
logit function
  using 92
loop functions, R programs
  about 27
  apply 29
  lapply 28
  mapply 29
  sapply 28
  tapply 30
low-level plotting commands 32

M

MapReduce 130
marginal distribution 8
marginalization 8
Markov Chain Monte Carlo (MCMC)
    simulations 51
maximum a posteriori (MAP) estimation 48
maximum likelihood estimation (MLE) 62
maximum likelihood method 101
MCMCglm package 57
mcmc package 55
Metropolis-Hasting algorithm
  about 51-55
  R packages 55
MHadaptive 55
Microsoft Azure 137
miles per gallon (mpg) 81
mixed membership stochastic block
    model (MMSB) 109
model overfitting 65
model regularization
  about 67
  Lasso 67
  Ridge regression 67
models selection
  about 66
  model regularization 67
  subset selection 66
Monte Carlo simulations
  about 51
  Gibbs sampling 55, 56
  Metropolis-Hasting algorithm 51-55
multicore 137

N

Naïve Bayes classifier
  about 85, 86
  model training and prediction 88-91
  text processing, with tm package 87, 88
neocortex region 113

O

OpenBUGS MCMC package 57
Open Database Connectivity (ODBC) 22

P

parallel 137
parallel R package 138
partially supervised GMM
  belief( ) function 103
  soft( ) function 103
partition function 121
PCorpus (permanent corpus) 87
Perceptron 113
performance metrics, for classification 84
Pig 130
posterior probability distribution
  about 38, 48
  estimation 48
  Laplace approximation 49, 50
  maximum a posteriori (MAP)
    estimation 48, 49
  Monte Carlo simulations 51
  simulating 79
  variational approximation 57, 58
prior probability distribution
  about 38
  conjugate priors 46
  hierarchical priors 47
  non-informative priors 42-44
  selecting 42
  subjective priors 44-46
probability distributions
  about 2-6
  Beta distribution 10
  binomial distribution 9, 10
  categorical distribution 2
  Dirichlet distribution 12
  Gamma distribution 11
  probability density function (pdf) 2
  probability mass function (pmf) 2
  Wishart distribution 12

R

R
  about 17
  data, managing 19
  installing 18, 135
  program, writing 19
RBugs 57
RcppDL 126
regression 62, 71
regression of energy efficiency,
     with building parameters
  about 75, 76
  Bayesian regression 77-79
  ordinary regression 77
reinforcement learning 63
R environment
  exercises 35
  references 35
  setting up 18
Resilient Distributed Datasets (RDD) 132
restricted Boltzmann machine (RBM) 120
Reuter_50_50 dataset 108
RHadoop
  about 130
  for using Hadoop from R 130-132
  plyrmr package 131
  rhbase package 131
  rhdfs package 131
  rmr2 package 131
risk modeling 45
Rmpi 137
ROC curve 84
RODBC package
  about 22
  functions 22
Root Mean Square Error (RMSE) 81
R package e1071 86
R packages 18
R packages, for large scale machine learning
  about 137
  foreach R package 138
  parallel R package 138
R packages, for LDA
  about 107
  lda package 109, 110

topicmodels package 108, 109
R programs
  control structures 25
  functions 25, 26
  loop functions 27
  scoping rules 26
  writing 25
RStudio
  about 18
  installing 18, 136
  URL 18

S

SamplerCompare package 57
sampling
  about 33
  from normal distribution 34
  random uniform sampling, from
     interval 34
sigmoid function 114
Simple Storage Service (S3) 134
snow package 137
SnowballC package 87
softmax 114
Spark
  about 132, 133
  running, on EC2 136, 137
  URL 133
SparkR 133
square loss function 62
stocc package 57
subjective definition of probability 2
subset selection approach
  about 66
  backward selection 66
  forward selection 66
subsets, of R objects
  Dollar sign $ 24
  Double bracket [[ ]] 23
  Single bracket [ ] 23
  use of negative index values 24
supervised LDA (sLDA) 109
supervised learning 62, 99
support vector machines (SVM) 71

T

Theano 126
tm package 87
topic modeling, with Bayesian inference
 about 105, 106
 Latent Dirichlet allocation 106, 107
topicmodels package 108
two-layer neural networks 114-116

U

unsupervised( ) function
 about 103
 parameters 104
unsupervised learning 63

V

variational approximation 57, 58
variational calculus problem 57
vbdm package 59
VBmix package 59
vbsr package 59
VCorpus (volatile corpus) 87

W

Wishart distribution 12
word error rate 119

Thank you for buying
Learning Bayesian Models with R

About Packt Publishing

Packt, pronounced 'packed', published its first book, *Mastering phpMyAdmin for Effective MySQL Management*, in April 2004, and subsequently continued to specialize in publishing highly focused books on specific technologies and solutions.

Our books and publications share the experiences of your fellow IT professionals in adapting and customizing today's systems, applications, and frameworks. Our solution-based books give you the knowledge and power to customize the software and technologies you're using to get the job done. Packt books are more specific and less general than the IT books you have seen in the past. Our unique business model allows us to bring you more focused information, giving you more of what you need to know, and less of what you don't.

Packt is a modern yet unique publishing company that focuses on producing quality, cutting-edge books for communities of developers, administrators, and newbies alike. For more information, please visit our website at www.packtpub.com.

About Packt Open Source

In 2010, Packt launched two new brands, Packt Open Source and Packt Enterprise, in order to continue its focus on specialization. This book is part of the Packt Open Source brand, home to books published on software built around open source licenses, and offering information to anybody from advanced developers to budding web designers. The Open Source brand also runs Packt's Open Source Royalty Scheme, by which Packt gives a royalty to each open source project about whose software a book is sold.

Writing for Packt

We welcome all inquiries from people who are interested in authoring. Book proposals should be sent to author@packtpub.com. If your book idea is still at an early stage and you would like to discuss it first before writing a formal book proposal, then please contact us; one of our commissioning editors will get in touch with you.

We're not just looking for published authors; if you have strong technical skills but no writing experience, our experienced editors can help you develop a writing career, or simply get some additional reward for your expertise.

Machine Learning with R
Second Edition

ISBN: 978-1-78439-390-8   Paperback: 452 pages

Discover how to build machine learning algorithms, prepare data, and dig deep into data prediction techniques with R

1. Harness the power of R for statistical computing and data science.

2. Explore, forecast, and classify data with R.

3. Use R to apply common machine learning algorithms to real-world scenarios.

Mastering Predictive Analytics with R

ISBN: 978-1-78398-280-6   Paperback: 414 pages

Master the craft of predictive modeling by developing strategy, intuition, and a solid foundation in essential concepts

1. Grasp the major methods of predictive modeling and move beyond black box thinking to a deeper level of understanding.

2. Leverage the flexibility and modularity of R to experiment with a range of different techniques and data types.

3. Packed with practical advice and tips explaining important concepts and best practices to help you understand quickly and easily.

Please check **www.PacktPub.com** for information on our titles

Learning Data Mining with R

ISBN: 978-1-78398-210-3   Paperback: 314 pages

Develop key skills and techniques with R to create and customize data mining algorithms

1. Develop a sound strategy for solving predictive modeling problems using the most popular data mining algorithms.

2. Gain understanding of the major methods of predictive modeling.

3. Packed with practical advice and tips to help you get to grips with data mining.

R Object-oriented Programming

ISBN: 978-1-78398-668-2   Paperback: 190 pages

A practical guide to help you learn and understand the programming techniques necessary to exploit the full power of R

1. Learn and understand the programming techniques necessary to solve specific problems and speed up development processes for statistical models and applications.

2. Explore the fundamentals of building objects and how they program individual aspects of larger data designs.

3. Step-by-step guide to understand how OOP can be applied to application and data models within R.

Please check **www.PacktPub.com** for information on our titles